BORN BY THE RIVER

PEOPLE OF THE MISSISSIPPI RIVER TOWNS

BORN BY THE RIVER

PEOPLE OF THE MISSISSIPPI RIVER TOWNS

RON MERCHANT

ESSAYS BY
ROSLYE B. ULTAN
BRITT AAMODT

LIMNER FINE
PUBLISHING

Minneapolis, Minnesota

Cover and frontispiece: *Mill City Morning*, 2005.
Oil on canvas, 24" x 36". Collection of Thomas and Katherine Miller
Half title page: *A Sterling Crew*, 2005. Oil on canvas, 24" x 36".
All other art is from the artist's collection except as noted.

Designed by Dean Olson

The project
Born by the River: People of the Mississippi River Towns
was funded in part by a grant from the
Minnesota State Arts Board,
through an appropriation by the
Minnesota State Legislature
and a grant from the
National Endowment for the Arts.

Lila Olson provided transcription services and
Cherlynn Merchant provided proofreading assistance for this project.

Maps courtesy of Minnesota Department of Natural Resources.

Library of Congress Control Number: 2005938175

ISBN 0-9776934-0-6
Printed and bound in China
Visit Ron Merchant's website at www.ronmerchant.com

Limner Fine Publishing takes great pride and pleasure
in publishing fine books supporting the arts.

LIMNER FINE
PUBLISHING

LIMNER FINE PUBLISHING
4929 KNOX AVENUE SOUTH
MINNEAPOLIS, MINNESOTA 55419
SAN: 850-0088

NATIONAL
ENDOWMENT
FOR THE ARTS

MINNESOTA
STATE ARTS BOARD

Table of Contents

TRACING A WINDING PATH:
IMPRESSIONS OF TRANSFORMATION ALONG THE UPPER MISSISSIPPI

ROSLYE B. ULTAN

From his footprints flowed a river,
Leaped into the light of morning,
O'er the precipice plunging downward
Gleamed like Tshkoodah, the comet.
And the Spirit, stooping earthward,
With his finger on the meadow
Traced a winding pathway for it,
Saying to it, "Run in this way!"

Song of Hiawatha, Part I,
Henry Wadsworth Longfellow
(1807-1882)

Ron Merchant envisioned a project to explore in his paintings the towns, cities, and inhabitants located on the shores of the Mississippi River. His goal was to inform and engage the local audience in the Upper Midwest about their own history, and to share it with a broader audience. His vision became a reality during a three-season journey in 2005 to eight locations in the project he named *Born by the River: People of the Mississippi River Towns*. Funded in part by a Minnesota State Arts Board artist initiative grant, Ron Merchant began exploring selected river towns that would in some way reveal changes in the landscape and subsequent attitudes of the people who lived and worked in these places along the legendary Mississippi River. Given the name "big river" by the Ojibwe, this mighty body of water flows from its headwater origins at Lake Itasca in northwestern Minnesota for approximately 2500 miles to the Gulf of Mexico. Artists have long been interested in capturing and recording its sublime and beautiful majesty.

In 2004 the Minneapolis Institute of Arts organized an exhibition titled *Currents of Change: Art and Life along the Mississippi River, 1850-1861* which examined the similarities in the collections of fine and decorative arts among wealthy patrons during this extremely productive and economically prosperous period in the Mississippi River Valley. One year later, Ron Merchant set out on a mission to document his impressions of Minnesota's river landscape through photography and painting. By walking among the residents of the towns and cities as observer and reporter, he gathered stories from local residents to learn about their experiences and perceptions of living by the Mississippi River in the present day of shifting social identity, economic and cultural transformation. Focusing his attention on Minneapolis, St. Paul, St. Cloud, Red Wing, Jacobson, Elk River, Winona and the headwaters in Itasca State Park, this self-taught artist discovered an underlying nostalgia, reverie and identity with the river, and the remnants of its fading prosperity in some of these river towns. The paintings from the series *Born by the River: People of the Mississippi River Towns* come to life in afternoon sunlight. Subdued by the interplay of heavy purple shadows that rhythmically interrupt the intensity of the light, there is a pervasive feeling of arrested energy and anticipation.

Within the stretch of one year, Merchant produced over one hundred paintings and photographs. The body of work is accompanied by multiple interviews of people from the different towns and cities to substantiate his thesis that attitudes and connections are influenced and shaped by place, consciously or subconsciously. The eight sites selected for this project are a stepping stone for Merchant's ambitious exploration of the 2500 miles of the Mississippi River shores. A similar journey was taken by the artist James D. Butler for his series of 14 paintings in *View along the Mississippi River* exhibited at the Lakeview Museum in Peoria, Illinois, 1998.

Ron Merchant was born in 1950 and grew up in the Powderhorn neighborhood of Minneapolis, the only son in a family of three sisters. His boyhood days were occupied with activities in the Boy Scouts, playing baseball, drawing, studying accordion and camping in the Boundary Waters Canoe area where he developed a deep appreciation and fondness for the natural world which developed into an attachment to the wonders, mystery and solitude of unspoiled wilderness. He spent time walking along the paths at Minnehaha Falls, in Minneapolis, and gathering sticks for camp fires, exploring sand caves, fishing with his father on their 14 foot boat and trekking across the old Hennepin Avenue Bridge on his way to DeLaSalle, the venerated Catholic High School on Nicollet Island. His connection and affection with nature would get passed on to his four sons who, with his wife and lifelong companion, Cherlynn Wellens, were raised in south Minneapolis not far from the city's lakes. From this background grew

Red Light, oil on canvas, 24" x 36", plein air

Ron Merchant's inspiration to document Minnesota's river history, the everyday phenomena of life along the river, the intersection of nature and culture, and ultimately the *Born by the River* project.

The desire to understand people's identity with place further compelled Merchant to pursue the river project. Questions that

Fishing the Levee, oil on canvas, 16" x 20", plein air

motivated his pursuit for this project include: What are the river town residents like, and how are they connected to the river? What changes have come about and how have they affected the people? What do the landscapes reveal? An interview with Merchant revealed

his quest when he stated, "I need to keep learning about places, about Mississippi River history and its people and my connection to it; I need to keep learning about painting." In other words this project is the first of a series Merchant will record about place in the landscape of life.

In 2001 Ron Merchant took an early retirement from his twenty-two-year tenure as a telecommunications specialist to follow his dream to become a painter. His career as full time artist, teacher, curator and gallery director started with two Compleat Scholar seminars at the University of Minnesota; one was a class on the development of French Impressionism, the other was on portraiture. Merchant's lifelong affinity to the environment and his fascination with everyday happenings of ordinary middle class American citizens in their habitual landscapes was finally integrated by the practice of painting. In keeping with the swift brush work and quality of light of French Impressionism painting, Merchant found a way to tell the stories about landscape and daily life that moved him.

The French Impressionist painters Merchant often emulates in his own work adopted techniques from the Japanese Ukyo-e (renderings of the everyday world) artists of the 18th century whose prints they collected. Moreover, Depression-era painters who depicted rural Midwestern scenes had an obvious influence on Merchant. The Ashcan School painters, in particular John Sloan, the Regionalists or American Scene painters like John Stuart Curry (1897-1946), Thomas Hart Benton (1889-1975), and Grant Wood (1891-1942) have, also, served as sources of inspiration as much as painters of the 20th century such as Edward Hopper (1882-1967), who depicted a landscape of existential solitude. From Merchant's studies and quick learning, he developed his own easygoing representational style with a hidden undertow that is immediately and quietly appealing.

At the heart of this exhibition is Ron Merchant's dedication to rediscover, integrate, and reinforce history. An equally important goal is to engage audiences with his painterly perceptions of the landscape. The journey behind the culmination of the exhibit began in May at the southernmost location in the picturesque city of Winona, Minnesota. The second trip was to the city he refers to as the jewel on the banks of the Mississippi, Red Wing, followed by a third trip to St. Cloud and fourth and fifth trips back home to Minneapolis and St. Paul. Elk River, was the sixth location Merchant visited before heading to the headwaters in Itasca State Park. Not far down the road was the last stop in Jacobson, which accounts for the eight trips completed over a period of five months. For each trip, Merchant loaded his van with canvases, paints, cameras, tape recorders and a printer for a digital camera among other vital necessities needed for immersing himself in the process of gathering information and materials to carry out the project.

Born by the River: People of the Mississippi River Towns was the perfect vehicle for Merchant to test some of his aesthetic and philosophical ideas about people and their relationship to place. As conceived by the artist, the project

allowed him to be outdoors for extended periods of time and to paint on site. Just as the painters of the Hudson River School, the first celebrated American landscape artists of the 19th century, Merchant tested his ability to record a particular time of day and catch the atmospheric quality. In addition, however, Merchant met

Tugs at Harriet Island, oil on canvas, 24" x 36".
Collection of Thomas and Katherine Miller

and interacted with the people in each community, and conducted interviews with them to document their attitudes and experiences. This interactive aspect of the project was Merchant's way to become,

11

even for a brief period, familiar with the community life. This integration with the town people gave Merchant opportunity to express a familiarity in his paintings so that any viewer could experience the same sensation of actually being there. Merchant accomplished this stylistically by creating narrative scenes of the town locals during the brightest time of day. He made sketches while sitting at the waterside or town cafés, which he then took back to his studio to transform into paintings of warm, unmodulated colors that he brushed onto the canvas with quick vigorous brushstrokes. Merchant has noted about his own work that

Green Light, oil on canvas, 48" x 60", collection of Robert and Kelly Miller

painting presents a *Gathering at the Landing*. Other images, such as the river in St. Cloud at Munsinger Park and Elk River's *Up from the River*, ask for pause and meditation. The richness of scenery continues with the paintings of Minneapolis and the splendid view of *Mill City Morning*, Saint Paul's solitary view of the moored *Tugs at Harriet Island*, the Red Wing *Fishing at the Levee*, and the beautiful bluff fringed city of Winona with two fishermen *Fishing Latsch Island*.

the energetic brush strokes and highly intense quality of light gives life to his paintings.

The paintings included in this exhibition catalog serve as a documentary study of the landscape and the people who live and work in Minnesota towns along the Mississippi River — the centerpiece of the third largest watershed in the world that was once a vigorous and vital engine for commerce and industry in the upper-Midwest. The paintings and contextual materials are arranged by each of the eight locations from the source of the Mississippi in Itasca State Park, Minnesota. The paintings range in content from one of young people *Stepping Across* the river to another which pictures a steady unfolding of towns heading south into Jacobson, where another

At the turn of the century, the Mississippi served as a superhighway for multiple enterprises and activities. As depicted in Ron Merchant's paintings, however, the river has been observed as a quietly flowing body of water and a contemplative place for a time of leisure. Often the river fades into the background of the community, ignored, set apart from the community. An image of an old iron bridge seen from the shoreline in the distance, for instance, connects one side to the other in the painting of a single figure at riverside in St. Cloud, *Reading at Munsinger*. In this scene, the river mirrors the shifting blue tones of the sky with a slight hint of overcast clouds while patches of sunlight hug the shore prevented from reaching the water by tall trees that line the river banks. The mood is pensive, but there is an air of expectancy as the trees appear to bend closer towards the water from an unseen natural disturbance.

Although not always within eyesight, the Mississippi is the theme that links the eight locations along the river that Ron Merchant chose to document, study, and compose into paintings. Merchant allocated three to four days in each of the eight towns, focusing full attention on one location every other week. It was necessary to return home and to the studio to collate, study, and complete some of the started paintings before heading out to the next place. Merchant traveled approximately 1,000 miles from May through September, took 300 photographs in each of the eight locations, recorded 24 interviews, and completed 16 paintings *en pleine air*. By being visible as a working artist in the community, Merchant believed that his presence would encourage conversation that would lead toward a greater understanding and appreciation of the arts. This idea was tested in the Nicollet Mall series of paintings completed in 2004, as exemplified in the Minnesota State Fair award winning piece, *Green Light*.

The post-modern era has given artists permission to explore the visual world without restriction or attachment to a particular style or direction. Artists today can borrow or appropriate images from any source, period or style, comfortably return to their roots, take time to look back, reconnect to history, and bring those experiences into the present. Today we are being lured back to consider the landscape, local and familiar places, experiences that are entwined with personal memory, socio-economic and political paradigms, known and unknown histories to discover stories that provoke and awaken consciousness about who we are and what we value in the natural world and culture. Lucy Lippard points out in her landmark text, *The Lure of the Local: Senses of Place in a Multicentered Society*, that she was intrigued by the vernacular element pioneered by J.B. Jackson, which finds connections between land and people and what people do there (Lippard, p.8). This is precisely what underscores Ron Merchant's project in mapping out

places of river town culture to find and identify the intersections of nature, culture, history and ideology. The thirty-five paintings, seventy photographs and interviews from Merchant's Born by the River project illuminate his story.

Two predominant themes emerge in the series. The first theme has to do with the perception of the river in the landscape, and the second, the impression of daily life in the river towns. Merchant made a conscious effort to trace traditional characteristics in the riverscapes, such as a body of water appearing in the middle ground of the painting surrounded by land or a bridge linking the left and right banks off in the distance. *A Spot of Shade* in the city of Red Wing clearly shows this nod to traditional landscape painting. The small city of Red Wing is considered to be the Mississippi River's jewel and is depicted by Merchant as nestled into some of the most scenic and beautiful bluffs. This particular historic location with its red brick Victorian architecture is known for its pottery and

A Spot of Shade, oil on canvas, 24" x 36"

shoe manufacturing, but the days as a prosperous exporter of goods because of its strategic position on the river are gone. The reality that he records of Red Wing is reflected in a mood of reverie and nostalgia in the piece *A Spot of Shade*. In this scene, a moment of contemplation in late summer at the waterfront with four figures seated facing the water while a noticeably sinister bronze dancing figure animates the ground in front of the river seeming to rotate towards the viewer, a contained winding path registers an intense yellow-green light otherwise controlled by the dark shadows of thick branches in the foreground space. Again, there are overtones of anticipation, detected in the muted, loosely brushed tones in *Up from the River*, an Elk River view of the water. References to the illustrator and painter of rural life, Winslow Homer (1836-1910),

and the mysterious recordings of urban isolation of Edward Hopper (1882-1967) are detected in these environments in which pregnant empty spaces seem to be about to reveal a disturbance.

The second prevailing theme in the series centers on the townscapes and the town activities, and is stylistically more vigorous, lively, and playful. These scenes reflect on the people's activities that hint at their relationship to the river-town. The townspeople are depicted out walking, celebrating special events such as Steamboat Days, and gathering at the community cafés or diners. Examples include *On 7th Street* in St. Paul, *Meeting of the Minds* in Jacobson, and *A Rare Sight on St. Germain*, St. Cloud. The painting on the streets in *High Noon*, Nicollet Mall, Minneapolis, focuses on the subject of noontime in downtown and rather than the architectural structures or the specific town activities the focal point is the prominent sunlight transforming the concrete pavement into a liquid yellow, and the lavender shadow in the lower right corner that cuts through the walkway. In *A Sterling Crew*, a group of young adults in Winona are seen taking time to share a relaxing moment, perhaps after a day on the river; they are placed at the edge of the picture plane which draws the viewer in close enough to feel part of the happening. This proximity is further emphasized by the diagonal thrust of the picnic table as it protrudes outward into the viewer's space. Sunlight dances easily over the figures and objects in this work giving it added animation, calling to mind the sparkling sun splashed, mid-1870s, painting, *The Boating Party*, by August Renoir (1841-1919). Merchant's interest and study of French Impressionism would have him well-acquainted with this piece by Renoir.

Up from the River, oil on canvas, 24" x 36"

A Sterling Crew, oil on canvas, 24" x 36"

City Morning, the signature piece, *Tugs at Harriet Island* and *Dog Walking Mears Park*, in particular, pose reflection on the implied narrative of isolation and containment. The architectural structures that frame the back planes, in each piece, impose a limited view of the horizon; and the sunlight that illuminates the foreground is, also, held within strict boundaries. Merchant's integration of color, form and pattern leads to a transcendence of everyday reality – a concept notably discussed by German painter Wassily Kandinsky in his writing, *Concerning the Spiritual in Art*. The visual devices Merchant employs, reveal his curiosity with isolation from mainstream culture. Empty space and light serve Merchant's intent to express aloneness as both reality and comfort. The content in his paintings shows the fundamental aloneness of life, and yet, the manner in which he describes this phenomenon separates solitude from loneliness.

Merchant's evocative landscapes and town scenes appear tranquil but more must be considered than the mechanics of the carefully executed nuance in the paintings. The configuration of light and dark patterns that have been empirically observed under natural circumstances dramatically reference profound issues in today's culture. Various pieces in the series, for example, illustrate Merchant's intent to move beyond the simplicity of leisure days in river towns. The Minneapolis and St. Paul sections of the series, including *Mill*

Light in landscape painting has, traditionally, been used as a transcendent element and a means for representing a divine or spiritual presence, or for that matter its absence. Such an interest

15

in painting looks back to the French 17th century landscape painters Claude Loraine (1600-1682), the 18th century work of John Constable (1776-1837) and Joseph M. Turner (1775-1851). Each of these painters investigated light as a dramatic force in nature from the study of cloud patterns to disasters in nature on land and sea. American art in the 19th century aligned light in nature as a spiritual entity, also, as seen in the work of the Luminist painters from 1840s through 1860s. An offshoot of the Hudson River School, the Luminists were a school/movement of landscape painters that worked in the romantic idealist tradition. Luminist painter, John Kensett (1816-1872), used elements of natural phenomena, such as sunlight, as a spiritual metaphor.

It is Ron Merchant's preoccupation with light that serves his narrative, and because of this technique, in particular, he may be situated within the continuum of the American legacy of landscape painting where philosophical intentions are bound with aesthetic inter-pretation. As Merchant matures as a painter (after all he has only been painting a brief four years) his artistic vocabulary will greatly expand and connections to the art historic lexicon will be more aptly made. Nevertheless, the painting, *New Bridge at Jacobson*, emerges as a culminating example of his position with history and demonstrates an affinity to elements in luminism, proto-impressionism, American Scene or Regionalism, and American Realist traditions. The piece was painted on site in the small town of Jacobson, a stone's throw from the headwaters of the Mississippi in Itasca State Park, and significant for the manner in which he paints the sunlight

with such intensity to cast shadows that spill onto the mirror-like surface of the water and the dark red-brown shadows lurking along the banks. The stillness and warm tones in the landscape belies nature's eternal restlessness, and yet, closer observation reveals suggestion of the early stages of land erosion, fallen and dead trees caused by the newly erected concrete bridge that replaced the old iron girder. In this piece, modern efficiency interrupts the natural environment and the future habitat for living things. *New Bridge at Jacobson* makes cognizant the vulnerability of the environment just as did much of the work of the Hudson River School painters, and the realism of Homer and Eakins.

New Bridge at Jacobson, oil on canvas, 24" x 36", plein air

It is not surprising that light functions as a predominant and defining motif in the paintings of *Born by the River*. Although a number of the works were painted outdoors in the full benefit of natural sunlight, the works were finished back in the studio with the aid of the photographs. Using the camera as a visual assistant in the painting process has many antecedents dating back to the invention of the camera obscura. Among those artists throughout history who used this technique as a tool were Albrecht Durer, Johannes Vermeer, Edgar Degas, and Thomas Eakins. The daguerreotype to Eakins was especially helpful in studying the movement and shifting of light patterns.

Light, without doubt, has the metaphoric means to communicate mood such as joy, sorrow, playfulness, and sobriety. Merchant mines every available aspect of light and color, the keystones of his art, as the quintessential expressive element in his paintings, coaxing and persuading the viewer to take the journey with him into the interior of the landscapes—as Longfellow beckoned to us in *The Song of Hiawatha…"'Run in this way!'"*

Size and proportion related to the spatial realization of the figure to ground are a few of the challenges Merchant has yet to resolve as a painter. This yet unresolved compositional issue is most apparent in the painting *Going Places*. In this piece, two figures riding bicycles are flattened sandwich-like between the flickering shadows on the shop windows while a couple on a bench wait for the bus. The speed of a biker couldn't possibly realize this amount of information with such clarity. Several other compositions further reveal the conflict Merchant has with the realization of the figure in ground. A confusing composition of intersecting diagonals and cross-currents of pedestrian traffic manifests this struggle in the two paintings *On 7th Street* and *Seven Corners*. Moreover, if Merchant intends to be representational in the style of the American Realists, he would need to carve out empty space in the composi-

tion. His challenges parallel those of other artists such as Winslow Homer, Edward Manet, and Paul Gauguin who struggled with the dilemma of being faithful to spatial and figurative perceptions. Nonetheless, Merchant succeeds in a unified composition with his use of psychologically laden light that defines the space and beckons viewers to become part of these electrified landscapes on the banks of the Mississippi River.

Born by the River: People of the Mississippi River Towns is a series of works probing below the obvious surface of everyday reality. Merchant's work in its varied moods and emotional states, exterior and interior narratives from riverscape to cityscape, mirrors the unpredictable life of the Mississippi as it flows from north southward shifting, as it twists and cascades downward, both in its form and substance. With the beginning of this body of work, Ron Merchant is yet another journeyman among the many distinguished artists and writers like Longfellow, Audubon, George Caleb Bingham, Seth Eastman, John Kensett and John Bonvard (whose circular panorama of the river was billed as *The Largest Painting in the World* in mid-19th century) who makes his mark in the sands along the Mississippi. These artists, each in unique ways, explored the depth, beauty, and sublimity of the mythic *Father of Waters*, which opened up America to the world.

Just as Longfellow's eloquent poem *The Song of Hiawatha* continues to sing and inspire awe in the wonders of nature and native culture, in turn Ron Merchant continues to document, tell new stories, and depict the changing relationships of ordinary people living out their daily existence on the shores of the Mississippi without majesty or pretense. Through the sensitive lens of the artist is captured a reverence for the everyday moment and an awareness of the power of place.

REFERENCES

Books:

Busch, T. Jason, *Art and Life Along the Mississippi River 1850-1861.* Minneapolis:

The Minneapolis Institute of Arts, 2004.

Coen, Rena Neumann, *Minnesota Impressionists.* Afton, Minnesota: Afton Historical Society Press, 1996.

_____, *Painting and Sculpture in Minnesota, 1820-1914.* Minneapolis: University of Minnesota Press, 1976.

Lippard, Lucy, *The Lure of the Local: senses of place in a multicentered society.* New York: The New Press, 1997.

Novak, Barbara, *American Painting of the Nineteenth Century: Realism, Idealism, and the American Experience.* New York: Harper & Row, Publishers, 1979.

Taylor, Joshua, *America As Art.* New York: Harper & Row, Publishers 1976.

Websites:

Robert Penn Warren Center for the Humanities Fellow Programs, *The Reproduction of Nature: Cultural Origins of America's National Parks.* Spring 2000, Vol 8, No. 2:

http://www.vanderbilt.edu/rpw_center/ls00c.htm

History of the Mississippi River and Tributaries Project. http://www.mvn.usace.army.mil/pao/bro/misstrib.htm

NGA, *Themes in American Art: Landscape.* http://www.nga.gov/education/american/landscape.shtm

Views Along the Mississippi River, James D. Butler. April 4 to May 31, 1998 at Lakeview Museum: http://www.lakeview-museum.org/pastexhibits/Butler.html

Mississippi River-Wikipedia, the free encyclopedia: http://en.wikipedia.org/wiki/Mississippi_River

Roslye B. Ultan, Art Historian, is a teacher, independent scholar and curator on the faculty of the Graduate and Master of Arts in Liberal Studies Programs at Hamline University and the University of Minnesota. She received degrees from Dickinson College and American University. Roslye began PhD studies at the University of Minnesota in Art History & American Studies and was awarded a Post-Graduate Fellowship from the Smithsonian Institution at the Hirshhorn Museum & Sculpture Garden.

Ms. Ultan lectures and teaches teachers in the area of 20th century art at the Walker Art Center. She also designs seminars for the U. of M. Compleat Scholar Program.

Her poetry and critical reviews have been published in local and national journals.

MINNESOTA'S MISSISSIPPI: A JOURNEY OF DISCOVERY THROUGH PAINT AND PEOPLE

BRITT AAMODT

Before the age of photography, traveling artists, called limners, moved town to town selling their painting skills in exchange for a fee. They would arrive on a doorstep unannounced, and if their services weren't needed at the selected home, the grapevine would quickly lead them to another. Everyone wanted a portrait done. A portrait was not only a status symbol, it was also the only means people had, before cameras, to fix their likeness in the world and save it for posterity.

Oftentimes, the limners would board with their clients. They might stay a few days or a week, however long it took them to complete the painting, but working fast since they were paid by the job and not by the hour. These conditions put limners in a peculiar circumstance: outsiders admitted, if only briefly, into the private world of their clients. They heard family stories. They participated in community doings. But wherever they went, they brought the fresh perspective of an artist interested in the uniqueness of his subject.

Ron Merchant adopted this perspective when he embarked on *Born by the River: People of the Mississippi River Towns*. Like the limners, he was largely self-taught. And also like them, he traveled in search of his art—he visited eight Minnesota towns from May to September 2005: Itasca State Park, Jacobson, St. Cloud, Elk River, Minneapolis, St. Paul, Red Wing and Winona.

"The idea for the project came about when I started painting on the Nicollet Mall," said Merchant. The Nicollet Mall is a bustling pedestrian mall in the heart of downtown Minneapolis. "I went out every other Tuesday and painted from ten until two. And that

helped me work out the details of painting city life and people. Then I expanded the area to St. Paul, and that was when I started trying to figure out, well, what did I want to do in 2005?"

The sight of an artist set up in the middle of a busy commercial center attracted a number of gawkers.

"When I was out there painting, people would stop by and start talking. Maybe twenty-five people every time," said Merchant, who found himself engaged by the people and their stories. "I started thinking, why don't I try to formalize this interview process? Do some paintings of a town, but also talk to the people living there, because I wanted to explore what Minnesotans are like, from the small towns to the large cities. What are their backgrounds? Their expectations of the future?"

Because of Minnesota's size, Merchant decided to narrow his focus to the Mississippi River towns. Having grown up in south Minneapolis, where the river angles out of a southeast tack to a straight north-south orientation, he had his own connection to the Mississippi.

"My dad had a 14-foot fishing boat," Merchant remembered. "The boat wasn't very big, and we'd go through these locks, which were large enough to fit two block-long barges. As the water's coming up or going down, you'd get a rope to hold onto, so you're not just floating around. The experience was like a science fiction movie because you're in this small boat, sinking down into a huge, walled lock until the water levels and the doors open and you putter out."

High Noon (detail)

The river had been an important landmark in Merchant's life, so when he conceived the idea of touring Minnesota, with the object of painting and photographing the towns he explored, he wanted to know how the river impacted other Minnesotans. By combining paintings, photographs and taped interviews, he hoped to flesh out a sense of place and time and provide a context for viewers.

"When I drove to these river towns, I'd check them out first. Try to get a feel for the place. I'd stop in and have some breakfast at the little café. If I needed a haircut, I'd go get a haircut. Just talk to people."

Like the 19th century limners, Merchant immersed himself in the communities he painted, eating at the restaurants, walking the roads, meeting the locals. He interviewed people in every town, using the interviews to give another dimension to his paintings and photographs, and to allow the residents to tell their own story in their own words.

Of Merchant's eight locations, Itasca State Park is the most natural, and the most uniquely tied to the Mississippi. The park's 32,690 acres contain the headwaters of the Mississippi, along with scores of lakes and some of Minnesota's last remaining stands of old growth pine. Merchant's paintings reflect the popularity of Itasca State Park with tourists and nature lovers: "River Race" presents a shorts-clad jogger racing along a narrow timber bridge, while "Helping Hand" recalls the thrill and terror of a crossing made by stepping stones.

Reports place Minnesota as the fastest growing state in the Upper Midwest, but the paintings from Jacobson, southeast of Itasca, prove

River Race (detail)

that sleepy towns still exist, if rare.

"There are two businesses in Jacobson," said Merchant, who drove past the town before realizing his mistake. "One is a convenience store that also sells bait and hunting licenses and the other is a bar. It turned out to be one of the most interesting spots I visited; I had no preconceived notions about it."

The artist was introduced to Sid Sarri, a hometown boy who like many rural Minnesotans before him had to migrate south for work. He only returned after retiring from 3M. But the Jacobson he came back to was not the Jacobson of his youth, populated by loggers and a seasonal roundup for bikers. A stabbing in a local bar put an end to the biker pilgrimages, while economic recession on the nearby Iron Range turned away families.

"This town is kind of dying. There's all these rickety places. And I wanted to stay here, but not with it looking like that," Sarri told Merchant about his decision to buy and fix up several abandoned homes.

"Gathering at the Landing" and "Meeting of the Minds" provide close-ups of Jacobson's reduced commercial district. In the first, a pair in billed caps saunters between the wood-sided landing and a single gas pump. Just down the block, a "Meeting of the Minds" takes place at the local bar and eating establishment. Neighbors settle in for a bite to eat and catch-up on local happenings.

Downriver, Jacobson's slow pace speeds up several notches. With a population just over 60,000, St. Cloud sits at the junction of the Mississippi and Sauk rivers, a propitious confluence during the city's mid-1800s settlement period when its waterways were used to mill and transport timber.

Catching Up (detail)

Home to St. Cloud State University and the Minnesota Correctional Facility, St. Cloud draws its nickname "Granite City" from local quarries, some of which provided stone for the state capitol in St. Paul.

As Merchant traveled down the Mississippi with easel, camera and tape recorder, he found certain themes tying the cities together. An appreciation for Minnesota's rich natural heritage and the friendliness of its people—the fabled "Minnesota nice"—recurred in interview after interview.

St. Cloud resident Judy Rotto used a German word gemütlichkeit, which she translated as "kind of cozy and still friendly," to describe her town. Interviewee Jeff Muntifering sounded another common theme: the overdevelopment and homogenization of Minnesota's cities. Sixty-five miles northwest of Minneapolis, St. Cloud has become a prime target for big-box retailers looking to expand.

"It used to be everybody walked downtown. You did your shopping there," said Muntifering, whose family founded the downtown bakery where he works. "But it's really not like that anymore. Now they shop at the mall."

Muntifering, among several interviewees in *Born by the River*, bemoaned the loss of the independent business owner and the individualized shops that used to pepper downtown areas. Though St. Cloud still has its swaths of riverside parkland ("Reading at Munsinger"), its historic foundation, located on St. Germain Street near the river ("Catching Up"), has given ground to one-stop shopping at crammed highway intersections.

The theme of overdevelopment is best exemplified by Elk River, the fourth city in Merchant's series. Once a farm town whose billboard announced it as a spot "where city and country flow together," Elk River has transformed into a faceless bedroom community overnight.

"Elk River is one of the towns that has missed the boat when it comes to its connection to the river," said Merchant, who chose the parking lot of Cub Foods to symbolize the city's transformation in "Carting It Home."

Carting It Home (detail)

"The whole city center has moved out of town. It has moved away from Main Street. It has moved away from its roots. It has moved away from the river to where the big-box retailers could build big-box strip malls."

Yet, Elk River's fate is one shared by many communities, both inside and outside Minnesota, as city councils try to juggle quality of life while increasing the tax base and providing incentives for business.

On the other hand, large established cities, like Minneapolis and St. Paul, have the difficult task of keeping their downtowns vital, as workers escape to the suburbs for cheaper real estate, taking their discretionary income with them.

The Twin Cities have taken steps to fight this exodus. One of the more successful has been the development of extensive trails running along the Mississippi and connecting parks and lakes. The Stone Arch Bridge shown in "Mill City Morning" was constructed in the 19th century by railroad tycoon James J. Hill for steam engines hauling freight in and out of Minnesota. Today it takes pedestrians and cyclists from St. Anthony Main on the east bank to the brand new Mill City Museum and converted warehouses off the west bank's Washington Avenue.

The towering skyscrapers of Minneapolis are absent in Merchant's portrait of St. Paul, "Tugboats at Harriet Island." Historic buildings provide a colorful and diverse backdrop to the white-painted tugboats moored off Harriet Island.

Minneapolis tears down; St. Paul restores, was St. Paul resident Inga Weberg's cynical take on the cities' different approaches to revitalization. Though born in Minneapolis, she told Merchant she preferred St. Paul for its welcoming atmosphere.

"It's just this big little town. It's big enough to feel like you're not locked away, and it's small enough that you can get everywhere and meet people… You meet people all the time in St. Paul who are forty-years old and have a house that's two blocks from where you grew up, and their folks still live there and their sister lives down the street."

The last cities in the series, Red Wing and Winona have capitalized on the idea of historic preservation. Some of Minnesota's oldest communities, they sprung up during the heyday of grain and timber exports and though still retaining a foothold in industry have emerged as popular tourist destinations.

"Red Wing and Winona represent the best example of people connected to the river," said Merchant. "Red Wing, for example, is a massive grain town. You've got huge grain elevators and trucks driving down to the river to fill the barges."

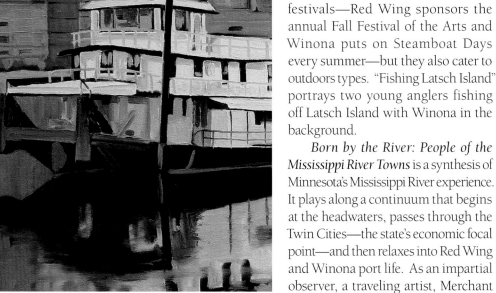

Tugs at Harriet Island (detail)

Also, both are known for their festivals—Red Wing sponsors the annual Fall Festival of the Arts and Winona puts on Steamboat Days every summer—but they also cater to outdoors types. "Fishing Latsch Island" portrays two young anglers fishing off Latsch Island with Winona in the background.

Born by the River: People of the Mississippi River Towns is a synthesis of Minnesota's Mississippi River experience. It plays along a continuum that begins at the headwaters, passes through the Twin Cities—the state's economic focal point—and then relaxes into Red Wing and Winona port life. As an impartial observer, a traveling artist, Merchant tried to express the individuality of each community. However, the interviews revealed a commonality of feeling, a sense of being Minnesotan if not being a member of a river community, beneath the differences.

Fishing Latsch Island (detail)

"The purpose of the whole project is to let somebody who comes to see it really connect to these people, and to think about the Mississippi River, one of Minnesota's major resources," said Merchant. "Do people have a connection to the river? Some totally not. Some, yes, very heavily. But let the person who comes to see the exhibit walk away thoughtful, figuring out how they fit into the larger relationship with the other people in Minnesota."

Calling *Born by the River* his snapshot of Minnesota in 2005, Merchant has plans to extend his artistic exploration down the Mississippi, eventually producing paintings of river cities all the way down to the Gulf of Mexico.

Britt Aamodt
Elk River, Minnesota
December 2005

ACKNOWLEDGEMENT

Art can be a solitary, isolating experience. I work alone, focusing on my subject and the canvas. Ideas and visions float through my mind and most are discarded as impractical or unreasonable. It was only with the help of many people and organizations that the small idea of painting in the Minnesota river towns grew into the project that is Born by the River: People of the Mississippi River Towns.

The McKnight Foundation and the Walker Art Center provided free web hosting and information updates through their website, www.mnartists.org, that connected me to the larger art community and informed me about possible grants for emerging artists. A grant from the Minnesota State Arts Board made the possibility of traveling to the eight locations a reality. They are an ongoing source of moral support and this project would not have happened without them.

The willingness of the people that I met during the project to share their time and open their lives to me is amazing. The twenty-six people that I interviewed contributed more than just their words, they gave the book its focus and humanity. Without them it would be just another art book.

Without exception, everyone I met working this project, whether they were interviewed or not, provided insights into the history and connections of people to each other, their town and the river. For these insights, I thank them.

Early in the process, before the idea of a book was more than a glimmer, Dean Olson provided a mock-up to test the waters of possibilities. His early design proved to be invaluable in expanding the project into a book format. His long hours and creative ideas formed the look of the book. Lila Olson, Dean's wife, was drawn by the project and transcribed the interviews from poorly recorded tapes. This was not a studio project and still she was able to bring out the nuances of each speaker with her excellent fingers and nimble ear.

Once the book looked like a reality, Roslye Ultan offered to write an essay to place the project in the timeline of art and history. Her knowledgeable essay gives the book some legs to stand on and creates a distinct place for this time capsule of 2005 to fit into the history of the Mississippi.

Britt Aamodt originally was assigned to write a feature piece about the project for the Elk River Star News. Her subsequent essay for the book adds a dimension of vitality as she looks at the paintings and people interviewed.

Norton Stillman from Nodin Press provided advice and inspiration to help me work through the publishing process as did Patricia Johnston from the Afton Historical Society Press. A special thank you to Susan Lukens for introducing me to Norton.

To all of these, I give my thanks with the knowledge that whatever errors or omissions may be found here, they are mine alone.

To Cherlynn Merchant, my wife, who proofread the manuscript and provided unflagging support for me and this project, I give my thanks and dedicate this book.

Ron Merchant, January 10, 2006

Headwaters of the Mississippi River at Itasca State Park

Itasca, the name conjures up visions of discovery. Huge white pines surround the three pronged lake. The Headwaters of the Mississippi River have been the home to Native Americans for over 8,000 years. Hunters with stone-tipped spears hunted bison, moose and deer along the shores of the lake. Several thousand years later, a group of more permanent settlers created larger, more stable communities making tools of wood, stone and bone. Today their burial mounds can be seen at the Itasca Indian Cemetery.

It wasn't until 1832 that explorer Henry Rowe Schoolcraft "discovered" the source of the Mississippi River led there by Anishinabe guide Ozawindib. He proclaimed it the "true head" and, with the help of a missionary companion, created the name Itasca from the Latin words for "truth" and "head": verITAS CAput. Itasca was born.

Within sixty years the area was being transformed by logging. The old growth pine forests and the beauty of the surrounding area were threatened. Jacob V. Brower, the land surveyor that settled the dispute about the actual location of the Headwaters, led the efforts to preserve and protect the pine forests so they could be enjoyed by future generations. Brower successfully pushed the state legislature to establish Itasca State Park and it became the state's first state park on April 20, 1891.

Today Itasca State Park draws over 500,000 visitors a year from all corners of the world to its 32,690 acres. Some explore and "discover" the serenity and beauty of the virgin white pines but everybody comes to walk across the mighty Mississippi River as it begins its 2,552 mile journey to the Gulf of Mexico.

River Race, oil on canvas, 24" x 36"

Lynette Butler
Age: 65
Retail warehouse employee at
Itasca State Park
Itasca State Park, Minnesota

September 12, 2005

Lynette, can you tell me where you were born; a little background on where you grew up?

Mm, interesting. I was born in Dorset, Minnesota, which, perhaps, you have not been to, but it has a reputation of, of its own for having all kinds of restaurants and only about eight people resident there. So, it's definitely a summer town, although when I was born there, it was...had a lumber yard, general store, those kinds of things, so it's a little town. Uh...

View from the Ranger Tower

Lynette Butler

It's on the bike trail isn't it?

Yes, I'm not a biker, but, yes, yes it is. That's where I was born!

How did your family end up there?

My dad was the janitor in the little school there. And... uh, my grandparents lived there. And...uh, that was just where they moved after they were married. Born in a little one room house, at home. Five of us lived in a room, house about this size.

And this is about 10' by 16' isn't it?

Um, yes. About.

So, your brothers and sisters. What did you have?

Uh, I had one brother and two sisters.

Are they still in the area?

No. Uh, brother lives down at Faribault, Minnesota. One sister in Texas, and the other one is down by Alexandria, Minnesota.

Okay. Are your parents still up here, or other family?

Uh, deceased, yeah...Mmmhmm.

Deceased. Okay. What are your first memories of the Mississippi River?

That would be after I met my husband. And, uh, he grew up in this area. This was home to him; and I wish you could interview him, because he has a hundred and one stories to tell.

Okay.

And, uh, I met him in uh, let's see, about '58, 1958, and we were married in '60. And uh, he took his undergraduate work at St. Cloud State which is on the Mississippi. But we spent our courting days in the park here, basically. In fact he asked me to marry him in uh, here in the park, so it's, it's a special place. And then, we live just three miles north of here on the Mississippi, or just above the Mississippi.

And how long have you lived there?

Uh, let's see, since '74, thirty-one years.

Do you have any kids?

Yes. We have two.

You have two?

Yeah. Mmmhmmm.

A boy, or girls?

Uh, one boy, one girl.

Do they still live in the area?

Our son lives in the uh...uh area. Actually, it's five generations now that have lived in this area. We have a great grandson who also

First Bridge, oil on canvas, 16" x 20", plein air

lives in the area. And uh, so we are into the fifth generation of living by Itasca and the Mississippi. Mmhmmm.

Well, what are your first memories of the river?

Oh, uh, I suppose the first memories were, uh, canoeing. (Quiet laughter) That's...that's what we did...uh, we canoed the river here and there and, uh, since we've moved back we've canoed it many times. And uh, picked, uh, picked berries along the river, and, uh... just enjoyed it. Thoroughly enjoyed it.

And this is with your husband?

Yes.

How did you meet him?

Uh, met at Oak Hills Bible College. We went, both of us, went there all three years. Then we moved to St. Cloud after that. Then we went to Canada.

Then you went to Canada?

Yup, five hundred air miles north of Winnipeg, we lived. And then we moved back, came back to, came back here. This is home. (Quiet laughter) So, so this is where we live.

What brought you back here after Canada?

Uh, well, uh...we came back, uh. He was going to teach. 'Cause he was, uh, he had a, a master's degree in administration. But, uh, when we came back here in the '70s, the jobs

in education were kind of scarce, so he went into real estate, and sold, uh, real estate out of Bemidji and uh, for uh, oh...twenty-four years I think it was. And he's retired now. So......yeah.

Thinking back to what this area was like thirty years ago, and what it's like now, what would you say has changed the most?

Oh my, uh...you know, I...I, we had a windstorm in '95. That changed, uh, you know, some of the physical parts of it. Took down some of our big trees. But, it stays so much the same. It really does. The river still flows, and, and people come and visit, and,

and uh, you know, it does stay pretty much the same. Mmhmmm.

You haven't seen a change in people?

Uh...There's probably more, uh, you know, uh, hunting land. People come and buy hunting land. That kind of thing, I suppose, changes. Uh, so we have more people that uh, are...are... have cabins, weekend places, that kind of thing. And, uh, farming is just about gone. There's a few that try to farm, but it's more of a recreational area.

So how did you come to work at Lake Itasca?

Why, I think I just applied, and the first year I worked here was, uh, '75. I've worked here thirty years, and, uh, and I worked as a non-tenured laborer at the, uh, Head Waters Gift Shop, not the new one, but the old one. And then, and then I took my civil service test and I got on, and I worked kind of, just about everyplace in the park, the area in the park.

Which job do you like best?

Uh, I like the gift shops.

The gift shops?

That's fun, yeah.

And why the gift shops?

Uh, I just...because of the people you meet. That's fun. Lots and lots and lots of different people from everywhere — all over the world.

Now, is this seasonal?

Yes, my job is seasonal. There are some jobs that are, are permanent, you know, year round, but my job is seasonal.

So, what do you do off time?

Well, uhm, It seems like we always, I... when I first moved here I had five different jobs to keep us going. But, uh, uh, now I, uh, it's just down to this one. We planted trees and worked fire towers, and did a variety of things. You do what you have to do.

Eventide

Helping Hand, oil on canvas, 24" x 36"

Fishing Dock

If you're thinking twenty years into the future...

Uh-huh. (Quiet laughter) I'm gonna be *way* too old by then!

What do you think it will be like? What will have changed?

Well, I hope that they have preserved the trees, and, and have, uh, kept the water pure. And, uh, just kept it as a place... I think Itasca and this area is a place for people to uh, reconnect with the Lord, with God and, uh, those things that He has made. And, uh, I just find that...I hope, and, and I know our present manager will do that, because he, he sees it as a place of rest, and a place to, uh, regain the things that in the hustle and bustle of life, we lose perspective on. I guess, that's what I would want it to be.

You don't see water skiing...

I hope not, no...

...speed boats?

Speed? The speed on Lake Itasca's ten miles

per hour. (Gentle laughter) I, think you can just about paddle that fast!

That's the whole lake? It's ten miles per hour?

Umhmmm. Yup, that's the limit. So, yeah. I hope those kinds of...the aspect of rest, and, and uh, just getting back to those things that draw us to our Creator. I hope that's what we keep here.

So, what keeps you here?

Uhmmm. This is home. I don't know where else I'd be! (Quiet laughter) This is home. This is our playground. We live so close that we come down here...you know, we pack up our little food and come down to eat in the, in the picnic grounds whenever we feel like it, because we live so close. Yup, this is home. That's what keeps us here. It's...I can't find a prettier place, and we've traveled all over. We just can't find a nicer place to be.

A little bit off the train of thought. But if you're thinking; what does art mean to you?

Art? I think it's an interpretation of uh, our senses, isn't it. Isn't it to capture those things we, we feel, smell, touch, uh see, uh, perceive emotionally...however... I guess that's how I would interpret art.

Do you consider yourself an artist?

(Laughter) Well, (more laughter) uh, not really, I guess. That is, I paint a little bit here and there and just play that way, but it's just

simply because it's fun. But, yeah, I don't consider myself an artist at all.

Any other thoughts or memories of the Mississippi River?

Mmmmm. Uh, it's not really memories because it's so much a part of our every day lives. I mean this is, uh... every morning I come to work and I see it and enjoy it, and oh, I don't think I ever come to work and uh, don't thank the Lord for this place and the way it's been kept. And, uh, it's just beautiful. You can (chuckles) hear the wolves; you can hear the loons; you can see deer. You know, just everything. I don't know what else we'd want. But uh, it, it's just a perfect place to be.

Well... thanks for your time.

Yes!

Melissa Rairdon
Age: 23
Gift shop employee at Itasca State Park
Itasca State Park, Minnesota

September 12, 2005

Melissa, why don't you give me a little background on where you were born and where you grew up?

I was born in Bemidji, Minnesota; grew up in the Lake George area.

Born in Bemidji and grew up in Lake George. And how many people in Lake George?

Oh, I'd bettcha, two hundred people. I do not think we have a population sign. So we're small.

How'd your folks end up being there?

Uhm, my grandparents on my dad's side are living there and my grandparents from my mom's side live in the Guthrie area, so they're just right in between there. Mmm yeah, a long family line, I guess, in that area.

Melissa Rairdon

And how far is that from Lake Itasca?

Ten miles. It's ten miles east of Itasca.

What was growing up like, and going to school?

Uhm, I love being in the country, I guess, so I enjoyed it a lot. N' some of... I lived on back

Stepping Across, oil on canvas, 16" x 20", plein air

roads an' we'd go four wheelin' n' fishin' n' stuff like that all the time.

And, where did you go to school?

I grew up, went to school in Laporte, which is about ten miles east of Lake George, yet. I have, I have...twenty or thirty cousins live around me...in my area. I grew up with them n' went to school with them. So I have a lot of family around. Still do.

So, do you have brothers and sisters?

I have an older brother and a younger brother.

What are your first memories of the Mississippi River?

Well, uhm...My mom has worked here for about twenty-five years, and my grandma (her mom) worked here for several years also, so when we were younger my dad would take us (my brothers), and when my mom got off work we'd go picnicking like once, twice a week–out here always and I remember and, I mean, I've known this area for, I...I guess, probably ever since I've been five. I've been here about, I'd say ten, ten, fifteen times a summer we'd come up here and go picnicking n' go across the rocks n' stuff like that, so...

Up at the headwaters?

Yup. Up at the headwaters. We'd splash and splash each other n' I have really good memories of, of the trails n' stuff n'

Serenity

picnicking around here, so... A lot of family has worked here, I guess.

How long have you been working here?

This is my seventh year. I started when I was sixteen.

So, still in high school?

When I started here? Yup.

Have you done any schooling after high school?

Uh, I went to NDSU in North Dakota for two years, and uh, went to Bemidji State for two years.

What were you studying?

Uhm, uh, physical education with an adaptive minor. I am actually about a year shy of getting my degree. I just got married two years ago and have a five month old boy right now.

Well, congratulations!

So, I'm putting school on hold for a little bit, but about a year to finish my degree, so...yeah.

How'd you meet your husband?

Softball game in Bemidji, softball game we, uh, his, my family members were playin' on it. He had some friends on the same team n' we ended up being at the same game a lot and started talking n' we got married three months after we met.

How old is your little boy?

Five months old.

What's his name?

Jeremy.

Kind of thinking back, do you have any good stories about the Mississippi, Lake Itasca?

Stories?

Things you'd do?

Uh, I'm tryin' to think...mmm... When we were younger our whole church would come up here on one Sunday a month n' we'd uh... they have a little area where you can have a congregation or family get together n' we'd have like a pot luck n' play games n' stuff. And we'd go out with the church. We'd go out to the... cross the rocks at the headwaters, play volleyball together.

Looking back to what it was like when you were a kid, and what it's like now; what has changed the most in this area?

It stays pretty much the same.

I guess, for me now, I used to think that crossing the rocks n' stuff was the most fun, and now I love going on the trails n' hiking. I see it a little bit differently, I guess, in my eyes. I like to do the bigger things of it, but I still, I still get in awe from the, the trees as you drive through. You can take it for granted after being here for so long. But, I mean, you drive through...the beautiful trees are just huge n' the area's so beautiful.

If you're thinking twenty years into the future...

Uhm, hmm.

what do you think this is going to look like?

Hopefully, they'll have the pine trees comin' back stronger than they have now n' hopefully it'll be really close to the same as my, is what I hope. I hope they restore all the buildings, they continue to do that. And, hopefully, more people will keep coming.

What happened to the pine trees?

Well, it started, this is going to be like a hundred year project to get the pine trees back, but it started off as almost all pine trees n' now it's grown into uh, our, our pine tree population has went down, decreased a lot. N' now they're tryin' to get it back to the original…so they're, they're working on projects that do that n' stuff. N' uh, there's prescribed burns n' all that stuff. So hopefully they'll get it back to how it was when it originated. That'll take longer than twenty years, I'm sure. Yeah.

What keeps you here, up in this area?

Uhm, family, friends, memories, I guess, uh, the people. It's a great place to work, 'cause uh, people are on vacation n' they're havin' a good time. And, you don't, when people are on vacation, you don't really have to deal with the grumpy people usually, er, you know, it's just, the people love to talk to you n' just tell you stories n' where they're from n' stuff, so…

So, how long is this, is this a seasonal…?

Yes. The end of May I start and then I'm done the first weekend in October.

What do you do the rest of the year?

This year I'm plannin' on just spendin' time with my baby boy, but usually I'd go to college. The last few years I've been in college, so…

They can work around your schedule for when college starts?

Yeah, yeah they will.

What would get you to move away from the area?

Oohoho it would take a lot! Uh. My husband and I are very happy where we're at n' we uh, his family is thirty miles from us. My family's about a mile and a half from us, and I have so many cousins n' stuff growin' up, er, all around that we've grown up together with that are like our best friends now, so I don't know that I'll ever… I'm sure I'll never move from here.

A little bit off the subject, but what does the word 'art' mean to you?

Art… I guess, usually I think of paintings or pictures, I guess. But, I don't know. It could be, uh, poems or letters or something of meaning, I guess. Something someone does that has great meaning to them.

Do you know any artists?

No. Not personally.

Any other thoughts or comments about the river, about the people?

Not, uh, other than uh, I love…I guess I'll just say I love working here. I love the staff. They have great people. The customers are always, for the most part, are just really nice people n' a beautiful area. Yes.

Well, thanks a lot Melissa. Thank you.

You are very welcome.

Susan (Susy) Teigland
Age: 43
Douglas Lodge employee
Itasca State Park, Minnesota

September 12, 2005

So, give me a little background about where you were born, where you grew up.

Right here.

And here is?

Clearwater County, I guess. Uhm, hmm.

How far is that from, we're sitting in Lake Itasca State Park, how far is that from the headwaters?

From the headwaters, twelve miles north. You're sitting in Clearwater County right now. It's…the line is right here between here and Beltrami and Hubbard. My parking lot is Clearwater, the other is Beltrami or Hubbard.

Where were your parents from?

My dad was also born on the same farm. I guess…

Do you have any brothers or sisters? Tell me about your family.

Oh, you got me on the spot. (quiet laughter) I've never had to talk about 'em. Uh, my dad's been on the farm, on his dad's farm, and his dad homesteaded it in about 1896. And they lived in the hill, you know, on the farm there, until they built their house and cleared the land. And I've been here for twenty-eight years…heh!…twenty-eight summers.

Susan (Susy) Tiegland

The Pines

At the lodge?

At Itasca.

Do you have any brothers or sisters?

Two brothers and a sister. My sister lives up in Alaska. She's a school teacher. My younger brother lives in Bemidji. He owns Honda-Yamaha. And my other brother is. . ., uh, has, uh, he's a rover, kinda? He means well, but he gets into trouble. (Quiet laughter) But he's, but he's the best brother!

Okay. So you've got some family that still lives around here?

Oh yeah, my mom and my dad.

What was it like growin' up here?

Peaceful. Secluded. I kind of hung out in the pasture with the, with the animals, 'cause I went to a country school. There was only two of us in one grade (sixteen of us: one through six) until we got bused into Bagley and then I came up two grades in cowboy boots and that was different. So. . .

What are your first memories of the Mississippi River?

Uhm, I'd say it's beyond good or great. It's like majestic. Always. True.

So, when you were a kid growing up, did you come down to Lake Itasca or the Mississippi?

We only came down to the park here like on the 4th of July for the family picnics 'cause the Mississippi comes through up north. Cross country it's only a mile and a half from our property. So, I'm on the river—river? Not *on* the river, but, you know.

Yeah. Not so much like Itasca.
You're closer to the river.

Right. Right. At Copper Pot Landing? It's really pretty up there. So, I think so.

So, as a kid, did you spend much time around the river?

Yeah, down by Copper Pot. They had snowmobile trails through the woods over there, and stuff like that, so it was a place, you know, just to meet. 'Cause they have a fire ring over there and, of course, the parents never went there. You know, so. Yeah, it was like freedom, you know. Always, always true, you know, I mean it's, it's always there. It never, you know. . . the river don't lie to you. I'll put it that way.

Okay.

(Quiet laughter) You know, but that's true, though. It's true, it don't, you know. It's very interesting. I still can't get away from it, though. Right now I'm doing a lot uhm, a lot of research. I took the Schoolcraft book and I read the diaries of the government, and uhm, the Indian guide, and the mineralogists, or whatever, of the government, and I've read, and I never did read. I've never passed a spelling test. 'Cause I *don't* read.

But, uh, my son was in a, uh, in a trial and society has just totally. . .I don't have, uhm. . . to me human beings, unfortunately, just about are the worst animal. . .on. . . See why I get in trouble? It's 'cause. . .uhm. . .they, they gossip. And they uh, think that they know the truth, and they don't know. They don't know how to get to the source, or ask the source without opening their mouth, and it causes a lot of damage. So I uhm, I just deleted everybody, more or less. And that's when I started walking the river. To find out the truth.

Well, tell me about walking the river. When you say 'walking the river', what were you doing?

I uh, I took what they had said and walked it backwards to find out the uhm. . . the uhm, mileage or uhm, where they had been.

Now, this is the explorers that you read about?

Yeah. And it, it says in there, like, how many yards back from the mouth of the Mississippi they had camped, or, you know, they had stayed or they ran into trouble, you know, or what they had found, or what they had discussed or discovered.

It sounds like quite a trip.

It's been three years of it, 'cause uhm, I don't know, people just think I'm. . .you know, 'cause I'm always alone, you know, alone, kinda. And I always have an opinion, but I shouldn't have. I should learn to keep quiet 'cause it gets me, like I said, into trouble.

But, it's just my own opinion. And I do, I do, I do believe, I believe in it a lot, and I have a lot of faith, because God's never forsaken me. He's the only one. People have. You know, so that's what's got me, got me into this exploring mode, you know. Just finding out the real truth about things. You know, because if you think that 1832, uhm, the medical world – how much further they have come. The space race – how much further they have come. And compared to what we know or that they tell us, which is great, I suppose. So that's why I, I uhm, mm, you know.

My neighbors, they were all farmers at one time and the neighborhood was alive with the kids and, you know, n' stuff like that. Well, now, it's, it's gotten to be real quiet, you know, but that's to do with gettin' older, I suppose. You, you know, n' me n' myself. You know? Things just change – a little bit.

How was it, what was it like when you started working twenty-eight years ago at Lake Itasca?

It's about the same. It really is. Uh-huh, uh-huh.

From the environment and a people standpoint is it pretty much the same, or what has changed since twenty-eight years ago to now?

Rules and regulations, I suppose.

More? Or less?

More. Yeah. More. And I've seen a lot of the managers come and go, come and go. . .you know. And I think a lot of people are

so. . .have tunnel vision in a way, like if you're, uhm, got a degree, or your whatever field you're in, that's just, you know, it's just your degree. It's your area. Uhm, it'd be nice, you know, if you could get the whole universe in per. . . perspective. You know, not just, you know, a straight line field. And then, you know, 'cause who are the new explorers? Or, what are they? You all have to have a college degree, er, and you're taught to memorize, memorize someone else's work. Somebody else's, you know, and you, you can memorize, memorize. But what about your own, you know? What can you add to it to further it on? You see what I mean now?

You feel like you're an explorer?

(Laughter) No! (Laughter) No, no, no, no, no. I just like to look at Mother Nature. . . you know, and see what any other, mm, you know there's a lot of unique things out there. A lot of things that. . . haven't been. . . you know. . . ruined, or touched or. . .

What do you like best about this. . .

Mother Earth?

Mother Earth.

Just Mother Earth and the reality of it all. That it can be all over in the blink of an eye. And you don't get that second chance to come back, and to enjoy it, but it can be all taken away from you. And what you seek here, here on earth? It's just uhm, it's just you. . .what you take with you is a memory. . .is a memory of what we do here.

If you had to look forward twenty years, what would this area be like?

In what perspective?

What changes do you see? Or, are there going to be any changes?

Yes, there definitely will be changes. Big changes. For some reason. There is. . .there's so much more here than what we know. So that's what I don't know if I want to publicize, because I know that there is, I know that there is. For some reason I can just, I feel it, and I know it.

You're talking in a spiritual sense?

Spiritual or environmental. We're the third largest river of the whole world. This is a, a source, okay? We have extreme temperatures. Negative below zero to summer, consecutively, for thousands of years. Okay, uhm, the trees. There's one tree that my son went to, uh, (when you go out of class, you know, if you're on a trip?). Over to Coffee Pot, they found some kind of tree, it's an old tree – twelve hundred years old. Or whatever, you know. Okay. Nobody knows about it, just, you know. Just certain people know certain things. That's why you gotta have that wider perspective. 'Cause you take somethin' from every field, you know, and you add it up, you know? You know, you take science and life, and just whatever, and you add 'em all up. And you gotta' come up with something. That's called life, I guess, you know. Uhm, now where was I? 'Cause I'm thinkin' way far ahead of myself.

That was my question. What do you foresee?

(Quiet laughter) I want to live to be a hundred and ten. I'd like to say…I, I want to say my privacy, you know, of respect for human beings. Respect for the other human being. Acknowledge and, you know, know not to cross that line. But that they do harm the other human being. And that there is good and bad. I didn't realize there was bad or evil out there… until just the last few years. You know, I mean it still didn't dawn on me, we weren't brought up to lie. Or why would I, 'cause you're wasting my time, eh, whatever. You know, it's a waste, and I didn't know why people would lie to you, when they look right at you. You know, I would take you for your word. I mean, why would you lie to me? You know, and that's gotten me into a lot of trouble. Big trouble, you know what I mean?

Yeah. Because some people didn't think that way…

It's, it's… a lot of people. But, I know that there's a lot of good people, too. Not, you know what I mean, that that's just maturity, I guess. But, uhm, there's so much here that…the earth doesn't quit spinning just because of us…or you or me. You know, it just doesn't quit. Uh, you've either got to keep going with it or you get left behind. And you gotta protect what you got. I don't care who it's from… if it's from the aliens or the government, our neighbor, or whatever (gentle laughter) you gotta protect. And keep it – good. The good, the good, you know, the good, the good will outweigh the bad…in time.

So, what keeps you here?

My foundation. It's my foundation. It's where I uhm, belong. It's, it's right. It's true. I don't uhm, have the desire to go away now, I,

uh…, you know, go and start over. Uhm, I like homesteading – for my kids to have a foundation, too, you know. It's where, it's where I belong. It's like that, the pine trees or whatever, you, you couldn't put a cactus here, and it wouldn't survive. So, you wouldn't want me out there in the real world. 'Cause I wouldn't survive very good. (Gently laughing) I don't think.

So you don't have any plans to ever move away?

Uh, no, I can't get out of Clearwater county or Bear Creek township. I've tried, but there's so much to do right here. There's so *much* to do that there's never a dull moment. And I even get laid off all winter, and I still don't have a dull moment. There's always something to do. I hunt. I've shot over, like forty deer, you know. So, there's always something to do, you know. You gotta eat, and when I can't depend on, you know, anybody else to

get my meat. Or, I don't want nobody else handling my food. You know, I like to prepare it, and grill it, and butcher, and take…just, keepin' busy.

Okay, a little off the subject, when you think of art, what does "art" mean to you?

Art? Art lets me see the world. And I don't have to travel to it. (Gently laughing) And I don't experience uh, that part. 'Cause I don't like to spend the time or the money, like if I was to go on a vacation. I don't want to spend half a day driving or whatever. I mean, it, it's a way that it can come to me, without me…having…me taking care of my own businesses, my own chores, my own life and family without having to spend the money I don't have to get to and fro. Or to, you know, it, it's a way that I can see other cultures, I guess.

Well, any other thoughts or concerns or things you'd like to share about the river, about your life by the river?

No, but that it can continue. Just like the river continues, you know, to, to run and to flow. You know, I'm sure there's…I'll guess there'll be rapids or whatever in certain spots or, you know, real muddy. But you keep on, keep on goin'.

Another Ranger Tower View

New Bridge at Jacobson, oil on canvas, 24" x 36", plein air

Jacobson, Minnesota

The main exit from Itasca State Park puts you on State Highway 200 heading east. Ninety-two miles later you meet the Mississippi River again. You may have traveled only 92 miles but the Mississippi has zig-zagged well over a hundred miles up through Bemidji, east across Lake Winnibigoshish and back down south through Grand Rapids to get to a blink of a town, Jacobson.

Jacobson is one of the two towns in the 30 square mile Ball Bluff township at the top of Aitkin County. Aitkin County was organized May 23, 1857 and covers 1,828 square miles with a total population of 15,301. Once a growing lumber town and gathering center for local farmers, Jacobson has become a spot on the way to the retirement lake place. A place you can get your fishing and hunting license and a six pack to go.

With only 72 registered voters in the last election, Jacobson has seen better days. But, there are a few people that haven't given up on it yet. A handful of scattered buildings past the abandoned Co-op on the south side of town lead you to the Forestry Station. This is where you go if you want conversation and a beer or burger. One of the two businesses in town, it's the nighttime get together hub: a good place to find out where the fish are biting or who is up to hunt bear.

Driving the two blocks north on 198th Avenue takes you to a town within a town. Clean, newly painted white buildings with red trim or red buildings with white trim on both sides of the street are a backdrop for a wonderland of painted concrete figures of animals and people. A family of pigs wanders down a small valley to a miniature barn. At the end of the valley you see the Mississippi. Several concrete boys are sitting on benches fishing. A whole golf course is populated with duffers hacking away. If you need a place to rest, there are a dozen picnic areas set up with furniture. This town has everything but real people.

If it's a nice day out, spend a few hours at the communal picnic table at the Mississippi Landing. The new owners of this gas station / bait shop / general store / liquor store are always friendly but not afraid to ask the new guy, "Are you an honest man?" It's a small community, so everybody knows all the quirks and stories about everyone else. A good place to stay connected.

You won't find a Wal-Mart or McDonald's in Jacobson, but what you do find is a lot more memorable.

Meeting of the Minds, oil on canvas, 16" x 20"

Sid Sarri
Age: 62
Retired 3M factory worker interviewed
outside his home
Jacobson, Minnesota

September 14, 2005

Tell me a little bit about where you were born.

Well, I was born in Detroit, Michigan, but my
folks just moved down there during the war.
You know, World War II, for the war effort.
And they come right back here. They were
born and raised here.

Where did you grow up?

Right here. That green house over there.

*And we're in Jacobson right on the river.
The river's in your back yard. Right?*

Yah. It's right below the bank here. There's
a creek goes there. It's a city block probably
down there.

*So, you were telling a little bit about how
Jacobson got started; and its connection to
the river?*

Yah, it started as logging. . .in the early 1900's.
The Swan comes into the Mississippi right
around the bend here. Logging camps and
logging got it started. That's how the town
got started.

How old were you when you moved back?

Oh, I suppose, two years old. That was just
for a couple of years during World War II.

And how long were your folks here?

All their life. They were born in Swan River,
right up the road. Then they moved here.
They lived here all their life.

What was it like growin' up right on the river?

Well, as kids, I remember during summer
vacation we'd just, you know, take the motor
boats all the time and go up the rivers and camp
all the time, it's what I got out of the river.

How old were you then?

All the way from eight to fourteen, I suppose,
during summer vacation.

Do you have any brothers or sisters?

Yah, I got a brother right there. He's workin'
now, and three sisters. They're all born and
raised in that house.

And the sisters? Still live around here?

Ah, two of them do and then one lives in the
cities in Burnsville.

What was school like?

Real good. We had a one room school right,
it's a half a mile up the road, that way. First
through eighth grade. We went from there
to Hill City ninth through twelfth.

Sid Sarri

And, Hill City's about. . .

Eighteen miles.

West?

Yeah, west of here.

Do you remember what your first job was like?

Well, first job I ever had I probably worked in
the Co-op store over there, stockin' shelves
and stuff like that.

How old were you?

I suppose about twelve, thirteen. That was
my first job I ever had.

After high school what did you do?

Okay, I went in the Marine Corps. . .four years,
and went down to the cities in St. Paul and
worked for thirty six years for 3M Company.

Oh! Okay.

Yah, and I retired three years ago and I'm
back up here now.

And came back up. Okay.

Yeah. I come here just about every weekend
anyway when I was workin'. Drove up every
weekend.

So how long ago did you retire?

Three years ago.

Three?

Yeah. Three, about three and a half, yeah.

*So, from when you were a kid growing up here
and what it 's like now, what has changed about
Jacobson, and the river?*

What's changed?

Yeah.

Yeah. It's died. It was more. . .as a kid this
was more boomin' up here than it is now.
This area has died compared to what it used
to be. Yah. The whole northern Minnesota
has, actually. That's the biggest difference.

Gathering at the Landing, oil on canvas, 16" x 20", plein air

So, fewer businesses?

Yah, there's fewer businesses. There was more farms and more people around here. There was even independent loggers around here, all kinds of them. You don't see them no more. (Other than that, yeah. . .) Even like the mines that were boomin' in them days. Like Hibbing used to have the biggest high school in the world in the '50's. Now you go to Hibbing, it's. . .just nothing left of it compared to what it used to be. The same like this area, too. It's just died. It was boomin' even around here then.

What's stayed the same?

Nothin'. (laughs) Nothin' really. Not a thing.

Well, the river's still there.

Yah, the river. (chuckles) That's about all.

Do you still use it? Do you still boat on it?

No, I don't personally, but it gets used a lot. Fishermen and stuff. They fish right by the bridge there all the time. There's good logans around the bend there, where they go in the lo. . .they're called logans, you know, where the head rivers, or the river changed, and there's good fishing in them all the time. Yeah. . .

Well, if you're thinkin' of the town and the river and the people here, what do you think it's going to be like twenty years from now?

Ah, boy, that's a good question. Yeah. I don't think it'll ever be what it used to be. Ah, you know, it'll, it'll either stay like this or get

worse. I think its best days are behind us. It was, it was boomin' here years ago.

And that was better than havin' it be real quiet? 'Cause it's a pretty place now, it's so peaceful.

Yah, it sure is. It's peaceful. Good place to retire. That's what most the people are up here now, is retirees. 'Cause there's lakes around here and stuff. They're all retired people.

What did you do at 3M?

Ah, I worked in the factory there on 7th Street. You know where that's at? In St. Paul.

The St. Paul one?

Yah. The mineral for the abrasives.

Do you have kids?

I'm single.

Oh, you're single.

Yah. Yah.

So, those were your sisters, your sisters and your brother.

Yah.

Do they have kids?

Yah.

So you get to be uncle?

Yah. (gentle laugh) Yah.

What keeps you here?

What I think keeps me here is just like the past. I had such a good childhood here. I just stayed here and then, and then come back to it after, you know, after I retired, retired up here. I think that's what keeps me here. Then I like the four seasons, except for the brutal

A Chicken for Every Pot

winters, they're bad. But, it's nice — four seasons. Summer's just beautiful up here. Fall too, in this time of year.

Tell me a little bit about your yard decorating project, because it's really distinctive and it looks like you've put a lot of time into it. Describe it for me.

Why I did it? Oh, I don't know. Like I said, this town is kinda dyin'. There's all these

rickety places, like on the corner there? And, I wanted to stay here, but not with it lookin' like that. And they, I eventually picked 'em up on the county auction, and cleaned 'em up and did I all this stuff.

Oh?

Yah. I remember a guy from work come here, years ago. . .twenty some years ago. He said, "This town looks like bombed out Dresden after World War II." 'Cause it was all like that one - a couple of houses down there. . .

Fallin' down a little?

Yah. Yah. Then, like I said, I started gettin' 'em on the county auction and cleanin' 'em up. . . doin' the best I could with it. That

Tall Tales, oil on canvas, 24" x 36"

house on the corner there, you know? You seen that dump? He wants 32,000 bucks for it. I'm not makin' that up. Isn't that somethin'?

Yeah.

There it sits. Whose gonna' pay that, for that? I'd like to buy it…get it cleaned…

Oh, and clean that one up, huh?

Yeah. Clean that up. But, you can't for that money.

Do you ever think of selling any of your places?

No! No.

So, you end up with a lot of storage and guest rooms?

Yah. Yah. If I sold it, it would end up like the other end of town, that's what would happen! (chuckles) Yah. Yaaah.

Where do you get most of your animals?

Twin Cities. Around River Falls and Anoka. You're from the cities. You ever been through Ramsey, there?

Yeah.

Yeah, that place. You seen that? I got a lot of that from him. The lights and stuff, there's a place in River Falls, Wisconsin.

A little off the subject, but what do you think 'art' means to you?

Boy (softly laughing), I don't even know how to answer that one.

Well, some people would look at your yard and think, 'art', like folk art.

Yah…

Just 'cause you've created something.

Yep. Yeah, that'd be the best way to put it is "creating somethin". I suppose, whether it's a picture, or whatever. But…

Canoeing the Bend

What memories do you have of adventures on the Mississippi?

Like I said, just as a kid we'd go down in a motor boat in them logans fishin' and we'd camp overnight in a tent and stuff. Those are

the best memories I have of it.

So, this would be without the parents?

Yah. Without…just a bunch of us, in them days they trusted us more or somethin' without getting hurt, or somethin'. They didn't even worry about you. We'd be gone for two or three days campin' up the river. Yeah, there's good memories, that's why I stayed here – good childhood memories.

What would it take to get you to move away?

Probably a tornado right through here, like what happened down in Louisiana, where it takes everything, you know! (Chuckle) You gotta start completely over with the shirt

on your back. One bad thing about here is, the winters are brutal and they're too long. …They last nine months out of the year. That's the only bad…the summers are nice and the fall, like this.

Yeah, yeah, it's beautiful now.

Yeah…Peaceful.

Any other thoughts you'd like to share?

Nnno, I can't think of any. Probably, if I'd a known you were coming in advance I would have, but right off the top of my head…no.

Well, thanks a lot.

Al Kauppala
Age: 41
Interviewed at old river front homestead two miles out of town
Jacobson, Minnesota

September 14, 2005

Just give me a little background on yourself, like where you were born and grew up.

I was born in Grand Rapids; raised there for… till 9th grade and then we moved to, oh… 4th grade, it was 4th grade. Then, ah, we moved back here, and this is where my whole family basically came from.

Then what happened?

Well, my uh, my mother passed away and, and uh, my dad got this girlfriend over here, and ah, we moved over here when I was in 4th grade. I started 5th grade in Hill City, but my whole family came from here. Where we're at right now is my mother's homestead. She grew up here. My dad was born down the road.

And, we're about two miles downriver from Jacobson?

Ah, we're three and a half miles on the highway from the intersection up there of Highway 200 and 65.

And, we're sittin' right on the river.

Oh, you're on the river; you're in the midst of it now.

What were your first memories of the river?

Oh, my first... hm. Oh, I don't know, I've fished that thing all my life (chuckle). Ah, me and my buddy, we were just catchin'... we caught a big ole' walleye down here. Must have been a ten pound walleye. We had to walk down the driveway here n' we was hot! We got a ride down here, and we thought we'd walk. Tried to walk back to town. Heck,

we didn't make it very far; we was tired of carryin' this fish (chuckle) so we threw it in the creek down here. There was a creek run through here, too. That come from Ball Bluff Lake that's just over here. It runs up this way and then it goes in the river up here.

How old were you then?

Oh, I was about twelve—eleven, twelve. He was another Finlander. A lot of Finns, Swedes.

You were telling me the family name didn't used to be Kauppala?

Ah, that's *my* name, yeah. I'm a full-blooded Finlander, ah, as far as I know. (chuckle) I ain't never been told no different, so! All my relatives are buried right across the road over here. I always tell my wife, "It *is* a short trip over there. So, I won't have to go very far."

So, where'd you go to school?

Uh, I went to school in Hill City. We didn't live here when I was growing up. We lived up the road; the intersection up there.

Is that closer to Jacobson?

Yah, it's... uh, that's Jacobson. This is Ball Bluff, actually, if you're on the map.

Well, describe your family to me. Brothers and sisters – do you have any?

I have a sister. She's twelve years older than I am. She lives down in the Cities. She's got a lot of nice old photographs and stuff that... pictures of the area. She spoke Finn when she went to school! She spent so much time with the grandparents— when she went to school she spoke more Finn than she...they had to teach her how to speak English. She's twelve years older than I am. So they did, they had to teach her how...They told my parents – they didn't even have a television yet, at that time – this is, you know, you're talkin' about '60s, you know, the '60s. They recommended, get a television. Have her watch as much television as she could, so she could pick up

River Rocks

the English language, because she talked so much Finn that she cou...

They didn't speak English in the house, then?

Not around the grandparents. She spent so much time with them, while I was twelve years behind. My grandparents passed away when I was just a little guy, you know. And ah, so I never got to learn a whole lot about it, you know. But, she can speak it, you know, 'cause that's all she spoke at first. Till she had to learn English. (chuckle) That's amazing to me. She's a LPN down there in the Cities now.

What did you do after school?

Run around. Raised a bunch a hell, and well I was a roofing contractor down in the Cities for a little while. And, ah... I got tired of that and I went to recycling businesses, and started driving a front end loader, and I got laid off and then I got unemployment, Dislocated Workers Act, or something. I went to votech up there in Eveleth, for millwright, n', and I got hired the day after I graduated, by U.S. Steel. I worked there for ten...nine and a half years, and, ah, I, I finally thought...well, I...it, it wasn't for me...it was like...uh, I wasn't makin' much money at that time, n'.

And, where were you living then?

Ah, I lived in Buhl at that time. I've, been...I, I lived in Eveleth, Hibbing, Buhl, uhm, I was up on the Iron Range for quite a while. It was a good time up there, but I wanted to come

back down here. Well, I come back down here and I started driving. It took an hour and ten minutes just to get to work. (chuckles)

When did you move back here to the river?

Ah, down here? This is...we've been here about, I think it's goin' on five years that was.... That, we came back. That was... Well, we had renters here for twenty years. We had a hell of a time gettin' them to move out 'cause they loved it, too, you know. (chuckle) Oh, yeah. Yeah, the first year they... I told 'em, I says, "Well, uh, can you guys find a place?" You know, I was gonna come down here and they couldn't find a place so, fine, well, "I'll give you another year," and boy, they still couldn't find a place, but I was like, anxious. I wanted to get down here and enjoy a little of this myself, you know. It's really nice.

If you're lookin' back from when you grew up here to when you moved back, what's changed the most?

Oh, heck, when I was a kid, when I was a kid growin' up, up here? They had two bars at up on the Riverside and Turner's Tavern. And uh, they were really across the street from here. And that's where Sid's strip is, right there? Where Sid owns all that? There used to be two bars there.

You know, this was a wild town back in them days. And they used to be wilder even before that, the stories I hear. You know, crazy. Heck, they had a Memorial Day weekend, we had a biker gang come up here and have big parties

and they'd just light a big old bonfire right in the middle of the street between the two bars, and just take over the whole town! About then they'd even... they just let the bikers run the bar and when the bikers were done at the end of the weekend, they'd just hand 'em a big pile of money and say, "Here," and...

And that was it, huh?

(chuckles) And they... Yeah, literally. They just took over the place until they got a stabbing. Somebody got stabbed. And uh, they were threatening down on Highway 200 down here a little ways, and somebody got stabbed out there. And after that, the whole damn thing, the bikers never come back no more after that.

What year was that?

Ah, it was in the late '70s. Probably '76, ah—to '78 somewhere, ah, I don't know. I'm not real clear on the dates. Yeah, bikers used to come up here and have big wing-dings. Well, first Turner's... Turner's was on the east side of the road down there, and the Riverside was on the other side. Turner's burned down first. It burned down, and ah, the Riverside, it lasted for quite a while. Contracted out with somebody here and somebody there, and everybody tried to make a wing-ding out of it, you know, and tried to make some money at it. And it, was, hasn't been too much... well, that burned down, too! So, that's where Sid, he bought everything up. He's got all that now.

Al Kauppala

He cleaned it up.

Yeah, he did. Oh, he made a park out of it.

Yeah, it's an interesting place.

Well, Sid. He's quite a character. Did Sid tell you anything about his history? I know more about him than he probably told you about, anyway.

Well, he's kind of a quiet guy,

Yeah, he is.

but he talked a little bit.

Boy that guy, he's a pilot and...

Well no, he didn't mention that.

Oh, yeah, shit, he's got his own airplane and all that stuff. (laughs)

It looks like he can kind of fix anything, though.

Well, I think he's a multi-million dollar man, myself. I think he's got a big ole' bank account. He planned for his retirement. He ain't never had no woman as far as I know of. Liked it bein' by himself. Some people like that.

Back from when you were growin' up 'til now, what has stayed the same with the area, or the people?

Uh, why, all the old folks, they all stick together real tight. The older folks. They're all pretty tight. We got a lotta... There ain't too many people that are really *from* this area any more. Getting kinda few but we get along with a few people from around here. Oh I growed up with...most of the ones I talk to, I grew up with an' went to high school with. Anyway, this ain't doin' you much good. (laughs)

Sure it is!
Thinking out twenty years from now, what do you think the area's going to be like?

Boy I'll tell ya, it's all been bought up compared to what it used to be. You used to be able to go hunt all over the place, and now it... I mean hardly anybody... the only place you can hunt where you got, you know, land, or you can find state land to hunt on. And I go around with my plat book and I can drive down old 65, right down here, I don't know if

Sid's Barnyard

you've ever been down there. It goes behind the back side of Big Sandy Lake and all of that?

Okay...

Well, I see people, they got land posted that's tax forfeited. There's people postin' land that's not even, nobody owns it! They just put 'No Trespassing' on there. Just to keep other people from goin' in there.

Oh, but it's forfeited land, so the state owns it?

Or county. County... County or state. But there's a lot of it that's posted. Nobody owns it.

But they don't really own It?

No, no, they just put a sign up. They just

put a 'No Trespassing' sign on it. Oh, that'll keep people out, but it's tax forfeited land anyway. You can go anyway, you know. It's amazing, it's all been bought up, you know. The city's expanding. People are coming up here. A lot of retirees from the Cities are all comin' up here. Which is all right, you know, I don't have a problem with that. They've all been pretty decent people around here, so far.

What keeps you here?

Ah, this land (chuckles). I've been wantin' to come here all my life. It's been kind of a struggle in a way, and I, I won't go into that. But I finally, ah... It was in my dad's name. It was my mother's, you know. My ma died, so it

went in his name, and he got remarried, and so it all got kinda tied it up for a time. Ah... Oh, he, finally...finally got ironed out where he put it in our names: mine, myself, my sister and my two nephews.

My sister had two boys. They live in Hawaii. – huh – So, I don't know if they're ever gonna be too interested in this stuff, 'cause they're makin' big bucks down there n' stuff. But I'm sure they want to hang on to it themselves. It's in their name, too, so...we won't tie it up in red tape and stuff and nobody'd be greedy and think we could sell or anything, 'cause that's not a big deal. It ain't for sale. We'll just keep it in the family forever, as long as we can hang on to it.

Someday the Governor'll probably say, "Would you get on outta there? I wanna make a bike trail out there", or some damn thing or something. They tried to do that a while back. They wanted to buy up all this, in order to make a *bike trail* n', yaaaach! You can't do that to people around here. Some people. Somebody'd want to do that after you have... on the Mississippi. I got a friend of mine, he lives way out in Swan River n' it doesn't really compare to this, but. Nah, I don't know. This is a beautiful place to be.

What would it take to get you to move away?

Huh! Priceless! (laughs) Ah, if I had, ah...if my nephews or somebody wanted to take care of the place for me, I'd go down South, you know, n' travel around. I've already been to the East Coast and the West Coast, so (chuckle) n' I ain't seen down South? I don't know. They need some help down there, they really do.

Yeah, they do now.

Yea, it's a mess down there. My stepmother was from Mississippi, so. She's got family down there.

Where'd you meet your wife?

She was my baby sitter.

She was your baby sitter?

Hnn, Yeah, I got a good story here for you. You probably don't want to hear it! (chuckles) It's got nothing to do with it. Yeah, my ex-wife left. She, she joined the carnival and left me with her two kids. The judge gave me custody of them and, that's why I happened to have need of, for a baby sitter. And she got three boys, and I, you know, me n' her, we got together and, she had her place and I had my place, but figured, well...we're spending more money runnin' two places than runnin' one, we might as well just join up...team up and take care of the whole works all in one place instead of runnin' all this miles up and down the road. And, so she gave up her apartment and moved in with me – that's when we were livin' at Buhl.

And their mother didn't...their mother didn't have nothin' to do with them for six years, and all of a sudden she started wantin' to talk to 'em and stuff. And finally they started gettin'

attitude problems after she started talkin' to 'em and they decided they wanted to go live with her. You know?

So I told her, I says, 'It's your God given right, and you're their mother," I says, "And if you're gonna' be a mom, be a mom. And if you're gonna be a mom then do it." And said, I can't take that away from them and if they wanna go, I'll let 'em. So, they moved down there. So we've had Anita's two boys. Of course, I call 'em my boys, too, you know. But, I don't have any children of my own, you know, like I'd really want to.

Any other thoughts or comments about livin' here, the river, what you used to do, what you're still doin'? So, what do you do on the river now?

Watch it go by. I have a canoe. Uh, what do we do? Like I say, we have our old party do down there. I wish I'd done more with it. There's lots to be done. Lot's of fishin'. Boy they're always fishin'. I can always catch a fish down here, northerns. My grandpa used to net fish down there. He thought people'd come from all over the place, the sauna was actually made into a smoker. He had racks and fixed a stove pipe out the sauna stove. It had a smoke hatch that he opened up in the back. I'll show that to ya.

Okay.

Oh yeah, he had racks – he could smoke hundreds of pounds of fish. Oh, he had a big old gill net he just threw across the

river. You know, it was... he got caught by DNR. (chuckles) They call that "poachin'" or somethin'.

They probably didn't like that, huh?

No.

Over the limit.

Yeah, he was over the limit, but he had people from all over the place coming in. This place used to be self sufficient at one time. Now, I got some shit, I'd like to show you a little... couple of things. Uh, mm

Okay. Well. Let's finish this and we'll...

The New Bridge

49

Reading at Munsinger, oil on canvas, 24" x 36"

Saint Cloud, Minnesota

Sixty miles southwest of Jacobson, the Mississippi River starts to widen as it works its way around Brainerd. Another sixty miles takes it through Little Falls into Saint Cloud. Here the river seems to get lost in the bluffs as the bridges start to jump over it.

Saint Cloud, named for Napoleon's palace outside Paris, is known as the "Granite City" for the Cold Spring Granite Company, the largest granite producer in the world. Although it is the county seat for Stearns County, the community straddles Benton and Sherburne Counties as well.

Of its 59,107 people, 76.6 percent were born in Minnesota and 91.1 percent have lived in Minnesota for more than five years. Median household income is lower than the state average ($37,346 vs. $47,111) and home ownership is also lower (54.6 percent vs. 68.4 percent). Saint Cloud residents have a strong German heritage (40%) while Norwegian (11%), Irish (8%), Swedish (6%), and Polish (6%) make up most of the balance. Although it has approximately the same 30 square miles as the Ball Bluff Township of Jacobson, Saint Cloud has 58,717 more people. It also has a slightly higher percentage of whites than the rest of Minnesota (91.7 percent vs. 89.4 percent).

But all these numbers don't tell you what Saint Cloud is like and how it got that way.

Founded in 1856, Saint Cloud was started by three separate personalities: a Protestant opposed to slavery, a former slave owning fur trader and a group of German Catholics who ran a sawmill. The sites of these communities merged to become one Saint Cloud. Then the granite deposits were discovered and Saint Cloud began shipping all over the world. The river was used to transport the granite and other goods until the railroads made it more economical and faster to go overland.

In the early 1900s downtown Saint Cloud was the center of activity. On Christmas Eve, 1921, the plush, 1,700 seat Sherman Theatre opened next door to the new, deluxe Breen Hotel. The Breen Hotel touted 180 mahogany appointed rooms and a roof-top garden. In 1930, the Sherman was renamed the Paramount and updated for sound. The golden era of downtown lasted into the 1950s.

With the expansion in the 1960s into the suburbs, downtown fell on hard times. A renovation of the Paramount in the early 1990s and a pedestrian friendly redesign of West St. Germain Street helped make downtown look better but by the time the Crossroads Mall opened, most of the vitality of Saint Cloud had moved west of the city.

There are still many great locally owned retail and service businesses and the people are genuine and friendly. Let's hope its a new trend.

Catching Up, oil on canvas, 16" x 20"

Jeff Muntifering

Age: 43
Owner Dutch Maid Bakery on East St.
Germain Street
Saint Cloud, Minnesota

July 15, 2005

So, Jeff. What's your last name?

Muntifering, M U N T I F E R I N G.

What kind of nationality is that?

German.

German, OK. Where were you born?

St. Cloud.

How about your parents, where are they from?

Mom is from St. Cloud and dad is from St. Augusta, a little south of St. Cloud.

So, you grew up here in St. Cloud?

Yep.

Tell me little bit about your school when you were growing up.

I went to school about two blocks from here at St. Augustine's grade school and went to Cathedral after that. The Catholic schools. Then I went to St. Cloud State, got a couple of degrees there.

Jeff Muntifering

What were your degrees in?

Music and speech communication. This is a family business and I just ended up here.

You worked here as a child?

Yeah. My dad started here. It's been here about fifty years now. So, and he started the business. And his dad was a baker and had his own business so, it's a family business. No doubt about it. That's it for my education, anyway.

So, are you married?

No.

Single guy?

Yeah.

How old are you?

I'm 43.

Did you ever live anyplace other than St. Cloud?

No, I've lived my entire life here. I have not lived in any other city at all.

What are your first memories of the Mississippi River?

I grew up, down here by Munsinger Gardens, so, I spent a lot of time down in the park. You know, playing down and watching the river. First memories, fishing as a kid, we fished there a lot.

Off shore at Munsinger?

Off shore at Munsinger and across the bridge. There used to be an old wooden bridge that ran across where, University bridge now, but, the old bridge, the Tenth Street bridge, was the type of bridge where the sidewalks were made out of wood planks. You could see in between them. Makes it sound pretty old. But, actually, it was there for quite a long time. And we crossed that and there would be a little holding pond, because NSP had a little plant over there and they had something to do with the water over there, and they had a holding pond, and we caught fish in that.

That was the west bank of the river?

That would be the west bank and the east bank, just down below the dam there, you

go down the hill. I'm sure people still do that today. That's probably the earliest memories I have of it.

What was it like in high school, was that high school age?

Oh, that would be grade school. We used to hit the Minnow Stop, which is across the river, not far away. Early in the morning, your parents would take you there and drop you off. Yeah, that's what we'd do with the river. That was probably my earliest memory of the river.

What's your connection to the river now?

It's through the park, I guess. It's more of a tranquil thing than anything else. There's not a lot of activity around St.Cloud at the river. There's not a lot of business or any thing like that. But, it is a good place to go down and just spend time by it. And we watch it. It's a powerful thing, especially if you've been to the headwaters and see how it starts and you walk across that and where it is here, I'm sure it's a lot wider in different parts of the country, but, it's pretty wide here. It's pretty solid.

I used to, as a kid or even when I went to St. Cloud State, I'd walk across the river to get to school. That's an interesting feeling to walk across, I know it doesn't sound like much, but the solitude is pretty nice. You hear the ice cracking, stuff like that.

Going Places, oil on canvas, 24" x 36"

So, when did you start working in the bakery?

As soon as your dad thought you were able to do something, you'd get a job. You'd start at a young age. There were certain things you could do, whether it would be sweeping or anything like that. He'd get you down here. I suppose, maybe thirteen, when I started doing some jobs. In the bakery business, family business, when they would teach you something, it would become your job. That's kind of what happened. Been here ever since.

You mentioned you had studied music in school, too?

Yes.

Still do any music?

A little bit. Not any whole lot. Not a whole lot of time right now. But I have a lot of good memories with that. A lot of fun with that. Played all kinds of music from jazz to classical. I toured Europe with the jazz band.

What do you play?

Trombone. It took me a lot of places and my instructor, he used to take out, he's a very talented man, a trombone player, too, so I got involved with him and got into all kinds of organizations and groups.

Thinking back to what the town was like and the people and the river was like when you were a kid versus now, what do you think has changed the most?

Down the Hole

It's gotten kind of commercial, chain oriented stores, restaurants, stuff like that. It's changed a bit. I think St. Cloud lost some of the identity that it once had. I don't know if that's, I've never been any place else, so I don't know if that's a common characteristic of all cities that grow or not. Maybe it is. But, that's what's happening in St. Cloud. Like you say, everybody's at the mall, well, it used to be downtown and everybody walked downtown. You did your shopping there, well, not so much anymore.

Do you think that's a good thing or ..?

Free Pop

I, I don't think it's a good thing. But that's because of the time I was born. People that are born now, or are fifteen to eighteen, probably think it's the greatest thing. It's their time, I guess, maybe more so. But, I still think about what downtown used to be like as far as the people down there. And what I see in your paintings, that's what I see downtown used to be. But it's really not quite like that anymore.

Now they shop at the mall.

So, if you're looking out like, twenty years from now, what kind of changes do you see in St. Cloud? (long pause) Well, how

about the bakery, what kind of changes for you guys?

We have big changes coming, actually. Well, this is a prime example. They decide now that the roads out here, that they needed to be four lanes, so next year there's not going to be any parking out front. Which, pretty much does me in. Yeah, the retail part of the business. Well, is that good, is that bad? I don't think I'm smart enough to tell, but, in my position, I say, "Well, I don't like the change. I'm not happy about it." You're kind of destroying this whole area, all these little businesses, there is no parking for them at all.

That's next year?

Next spring. And my viewpoint is that I don't understand why they encourage that. They could encourage all small businesses like this, up and down the street and help them flourish. But, just to take the parking away and let everybody sort of flounder, seems to be more of their course of action. You either have to move and that's not easy because, you know, this isn't a million dollar operation, obviously. So, to pay for what real estate costs now days, what building costs now days, fees for this, that, it's going to be hard to do. Not impossible, but hard to do.

I can see why a lot of people don't do it. Most people don't do it. That's the changes going on in St. Cloud, I guess. Like I say, is it good? That's their position here, I guess. Younger people probably don't have the connection

A Rare Sight on St. Germain, oil on canvas, 16" x 20", plein air

Ladies Handbags

Man with the Donuts

to me. It's what you see in your eye is art. Any type of a body movement, I guess, or nature. It can be pretty much whatever you want it to be. Sometimes it goes overboard, too. Anyway, that's it, I guess.

So, are you still playing trombone?

I still play a little bit but not really with any group. I don't have a whole lot of time. That's something that when the embrasure gets weak, the chops kind of go and that's kind of it. And there's other people out there that are more qualified to play.

Do you play any other instruments?

Pretty much that one. I mean I can tinker around on the piano and guitar. I would never say that I was, I play for myself.

Well, any other thoughts or comments you would like to share?

I think St. Cloud is a good city, I just think that it is going through a lot of changes right now that, it will be interesting to see twenty years from now. I'm not sure what the place will be like. It seems to be getting very busy, a lot more people. I know the outskirts are all being developed with housing and stuff like that and I know the road structure is probably, aren't the best, I don't know if you've been up and down Division Street or not, but, it's tough. When you hit every stop light, it's going to take awhile. Well, from when I got my license to what it is now, it's quite different.

that we do or some of the older people do and it doesn't affect them as much.

How long has the bakery been here?

Forty-nine years, this year.

And it was started by your dad?

Yes.

What's his name?

Robert, Bob.

The bakery and family. Are the family still living here in town?

Yeah, my mom still lives here in town. We all, all my family's here in town. I have three sisters. One works in St. Benedict's Center which is a nursing home. She also works here a lot too. I have a brother that works at Cub

Foods here in St. Cloud and I have another sister that works at Nextel.

So, do you ever see yourself moving away from St. Cloud? Or, what would it take to make you move?

You know, that's a good question because, yeah, I could, only that I never have before. And like I say, if this whole road thing kind of affects us to the point where I got to, maybe do have to, it wouldn't be far, if I kept the business, I might go to Sauk Rapids, something like that. I don't think moving completely out of the state, probably too old for that. Pack anymore, sounds tiring.

So, kind of off the subject, when you think of art, what does that mean to you?

Art? Just the whole big picture. It's such a wide..., painting, music, dance, sculpting. Art, painting, a very personal thing, I guess

Debbie Johnson
Age: 53
Gateway Motel desk manager
Saint Cloud, Minnesota

July 15, 2005

Debbie, where were you born?

Here in St. Cloud.

And your family, where are they from?

My father was born and raised here in St. Cloud and my mother was born in Albany which is about twenty miles west of here.

Tell me a little bit about growing up in St. Cloud.

As far as what?

Schools, friends...What was it like being a kid in St. Cloud?

Just your average childhood, you know. I

went to school up here at St. Augustine's which is just a couple blocks up the street. Went to high school at Tech. Went on to vocational school here in St. Cloud, also.

Have you ever lived any place other than St. Cloud?

No, it's always been St. Cloud.

Married? Got a family of your own?

Married. We have no children, but my husband was born in Sauk Center and lived most of his life here in St. Cloud.

How'd you meet your husband?

On the job. I was a taxi dispatcher and he was a taxi driver.

And how long ago was that?

We met back in 1980. Actually, we went to high school together but never knew each other. We both went to the same high school. I knew who he was from seeing him but never knew him personally until we started working together.

What kind of things were you interested in, in high school?

Basically just hanging out with my friends and having a good time.

But, a different group of friends?

Oh yeah, totally. Yep. Him and I had totally different. I was not interested in boys and he wasn't interested in girls.

So you had to wait a little bit.

Yeah, we weren't ready to have boy friends and girl friends, you know. It wasn't until I got older I got interested in boys (laughs). Same thing with him, too. You date but, it was nothing. Nothing, friendly. It was nothing until we got older, got more mature, I guess.

You're not at the taxi company anymore, so, what happened? Is he still at the taxi company?

He is still driving.

He is? OK.

Yes, he is, as a matter of fact. He's been there like 30 years.

So he must know St. Cloud pretty well.

Yes, he does. There's not much that he doesn't know about the area, as far as driving.

Well, when you think of the Mississippi River, what are your youngest thoughts of what that was? Any memories of that?

I have absolutely no memories of the river. It's always been there and I just never thought

much about it. What impressed me about the river, when I got older, I had the chance to go up to Itasca and see the headwaters. And at that, I was amazed with that. To see how the river actually started to flow from this little trickle and then becomes the mighty Mississippi. So that impressed me in my adult life. But as far as living by the river...

Never did any fishing or boating?

No. No. I mean it's always been there. I cross it going back and forth from work and that's kind of it. Yeah.

So, if you're thinking back to St. Cloud, what it was like when you were growing up, to what it's become now (the growth, the number of people, how people interact with each other), what has changed the most?

St. Cloud has really, really grown over the years. A lot of changes. I don't know, I don't think people are as, maybe as friendly. It's getting so big. Getting too much like the Twin Cities area. I think it's kind of losing a small town atmosphere because it's getting so big and so sprawled out. That would be my observation from when I was a child.

Are many of your friends still here from high school?

A few. Yes.

Do you still stay connected to them?

Yes, I have.

Debbie Johnson

If you're looking twenty years out in the future, what do you think, what do you foresee St. Cloud becoming?

I think St. Cloud is going to end up being, the way the growth is going, I think it's going to be connected onto the Twin Cities. Be a suburb of the Twin Cities.

So, will that be a good thing or a bad thing?

I don't think it's going to be, in my opinion, it's not going to be the best because, when you lose your small town flavor, things just become, like, St. Cloud now has more crime and stuff. When I was a kid, you could leave your doors unlocked, not have to worry about anything. Heck, now they're breaking into homes right and left when people are home sleeping. So I think the bigger you get, the more problems with that. And, I think that's going to be bad for St. Cloud.

What keeps you here in St. Cloud? What has kept you here all these years?

I do like St. Cloud's location. Even though St. Cloud is growing, St. Cloud is close enough to the Cities where if you want to go to a concert, you're not that far away. Or other things down in the Cities, other sporting events or whatever, you're close enough where you can drive to it. Yet, you're far enough away from that big city atmosphere, which I don't like. I like the smaller town atmosphere, which St. Cloud is kind of losing with it's growth.

What would it take to get you to move away?

I have never thought about moving away. If circumstances were to arise where I had to, it would be OK. I mean it wouldn't bother me to move. But I've no plans to move.

So, your cemetery is going to be here in St.

St. Augustine

Cloud someplace?

Probably. Probably, probably, yes.

One other question, a little off the path, when you think of art, what does that mean to you?

I enjoy looking at people's art. Like your stuff that you showed me the other day, I think is just beautiful. I enjoy observing people's art. I, myself, am not at all artistic in any shape or form (laughs). So, when I see somebody's talent, such as yours, I really can appreciate it because it takes a real talent to do stuff like that. So I do enjoy it.

Do you know any artists?

You're the only one.

So, that's it. Well, that's part of this project, to get people to know artists. So, it must be working.

It's very nice meeting you because I do appreciate people's abilities like that.

Any other thoughts or comments?

Not that I can think of, Ron.

Not the Crossroads Mall

Judy Rotto
Age: 54
Teacher interviewed downtown on St. Germain and 5th
Saint Cloud, Minnesota

July 13, 2005

Judy, from St. Cloud?

From St. Cloud. I was born in Mankato. But I'd say St. Cloud is my home since 1972.

Did you come up with your family, or how did you come up to St. Cloud?

Well, actually, I graduated from college in Moorhead and I came to be a teacher. So, I think that I guess this is my adult home, my adult birthplace. And my parents are both from Rapidan, which is a little tiny town outside of Mankato.

Still Minnesota, though.

Still Minnesota.

Is Rotto, what kind of name?

Rotto is actually Norwegian. My husband's family is from a little island in Norway. You wouldn't think it, because it sounds kind of Italian, but it was Rottone but they changed it.

Judy Rotto

How did you meet your husband?

In high school, sweethearts from Fergus Falls. Student council, decorating the homecoming float. And we were best friends first, then we fell in love. So, 1971 we were married the winter before we came here.

Have any kids?

We have two sons. Karl is twenty today and that's who's birthday we were celebrating. And then Isaac is twenty-two.

In college, did you go straight into education?

Yes, I always knew I was going to be a teacher. Always. I was thinking music, because I love music so much, but the Concordia program of ear training and all that intense study made me so nervous. I have a piano, though, in my classroom and I've been a kindergarten through third grade teacher for 33 years.

Wow.

I know it. I can't believe it!

Do you do any art, other than the music?

Other than the music, I love to write letters. I don't know if that's really art. I love to write and I love to go to plays and hear musical performances. I am an art appreciator. I play the piano. I played since I was in second grade. I had lessons through high school. So, that's my piece.

What were your first memories of the Mississippi River?

I'd have to say, spelling it in school. (laughs) And imaging the beginning of the river all the way down through the country. I'd say the incredible river. Going to the headwaters when we were little, that was really important. And the next, well, Mark Twain, Tom Sawyer, Mark Twain. And then I'd have to say coming here and actually living within six blocks of the

river. We cross it every day, several times. So I think that, I never thought I would like this area because we were always in small towns, Norwegian roots kind of places, and we came to St. Cloud and we thought, "Well, we'll stay here for a couple of years." And, here we are, it's our home. We love it.

So, how long have you been in St. Cloud, then?

1972. Thirty-three years. As long as I've been teaching.

What was it like back then, that it isn't now, from the terms of people?

I would have to say that there is a distinct feeling of someone who's been a St. Cloud person all their life. But then, in the last 15 – 20 years, there've been so many wonderful new people to come. And, then the fact that it's a college town with the University close by, and my husband is at the University, so it's a, I think it's growing and it's changing and it's

Vals Hamburgers

getting to be more urban. And I think more people are coming here from bigger cities, different places. It's more diverse now. When I first taught, I had 32 children in third grade and all but one was Catholic and white. And now, I have 20 to 26 children and I'd say 8 to 10 are children of color. So, it's almost like one-third are of color which brings a wonderful flavor to any community. Kids of all nations. So, as far as our changes, we were welcomed by a community of teaching professionals and also neighbors, and that made it feel like home.

How did you decide on St. Cloud after college?

That was where my job was and I wanted to teach so badly, so, the beginning of August, I was hired at the last minute. In those days, that year especially, there were so many candidates for teaching and not as many jobs. So, I was very lucky. There were two thousand people interviewing for this job, and I was one of the last to be named. That was great.

Well, if you're thinking, looking towards the future, what do you think the changes in St. Cloud will be like twenty years from now?

Well I hope it stays. We have a word in German called "gemutlichkeit", which means "kind of cozy and still friendly" and I hope it stays. Even for a big city where you can walk and say "Hello", meet people and care for neighbors. From the bigness, because I know that border from Minneapolis to St. Cloud is like I-94 is compressed.

It's compressed a lot, especially, what are the thoughts about the light rail coming in?

Oh, I'd love it. That would be so wonderful. We wouldn't have to drive individually. It would help the congestion. Make it more convenient. A lot of people do live here and work there, and vice versa.

So, any plans to move away?

No, no plans to move away. We were talking about selling our bigger home now because we're getting ready to think about retirement down the road. We also have two nice sons and this is their home and they don't want us to think about that.

They're still in St. Cloud?

Actually, they go to school in St. Paul. My youngest was in Boson last year but he's going to Hamline. And, then our oldest, Isaac, is at Macalester. They both love St. Paul. So, they're just an hour away.

Just enough they can bring the laundry home.

Yes, you know it.

Yeah, I raised four boys and they have a tendency to do that. So, when retiring, you going to live and die here?

Probably, probably. We really like it here. I haven't been thinking of retirement, but I probably should, I'm getting close. But I still love what I do.

And what grades do you teach?

Walking the River

Right now I'm in first grade. But, I've been a K through three teacher, so I guess you would really call me a primary teacher. And I have done some teaching at the University and I took some time out to do some teaching-the-teachers, the other side of the brain. Enthusiasm and motivation and putting in cooking and music and walks and bus rides downtown, and all that into, call it "human being learning".

Well, any other nice stories or thoughts about St. Cloud or the river?

Well, St. Cloud has, teaching kindergarten, I got to know, and actually an artist's daughter, Bela Petheo. I got to teach his sweet, sweet daughter. And he gave me a beautiful print that hangs above my bed.

And so, that welcome was wonderful and knowing about his life and what he did. And, I live so close to the Munsinger Garden, the flowers there are just incredible. We have a connection to it, Germans don't, we lived away with a foreign exchange student there for awhile and we, but we're like family. So, one winter, about four years ago, we walked on the ice of the Mississippi River. That was an incredible experience. The river is just, flowing, ebbing. We've been kind of grateful to be here.

Well, that kind of wraps this up for a little bit. That was pretty painless.

That was pretty painless. You were a wonderful man to talk to.

Up from the River, oil on canvas, 24" x 36"

Elk River

Driving St. Germain east across the river past the Dutch Maid Bakery in Saint Cloud will take you to Highway 10. Southeast thirty-five miles as Highway 10 follows the Mississippi brings you to present-day Elk River, a thriving 21st century city trying to regain its roots.

In the late 1700s, the area was a natural boundary between rival Dakota and Ojibwe nations. In 1772 and again in 1773 battles were fought between these enemies where the Elk River meets the Mississippi. The area was ceded by the tribes to the United States in 1837. By 1846 a trading post had been built and the population started to grow. In 1872, the Village of Elk River had over 2,000 people and became the Sherburne County seat.

After several fires burned through the old State Street business center in 1898, a new "Brick Block" was built and is now considered the historic downtown area of Elk River.

With the construction of Interstate 94 and the relocation of Highway 169, business life moved out of downtown to the 169 corridor. Here highway access and large open fields yielded to the "big-box" retailers. Wal-Mart, Target, Home Depot and Cub Foods drew shoppers from the surrounding area and away from the historic downtown businesses. But, once again, fire played a part in Elk River's history. A fire destroyed one of the buildings on Main Street and opened up a view of the forgotten Mississippi River.

After years of discussion and inaction, a plan is in place to once again start taking advantage of the natural wonder of the Mississippi at Elk River. Rivers Edge Park will be located where the fire created some green space and will consist of four levels that step down to the river. The concept also includes a downtown square and an amphitheater over-looking the river.

While per capita income is around the national average of $21,587 (Elk River: $21,808), median household income at $58,114 is well above the Minnesota median ($47,111) and the national median household income of $41,994. This can be explained by the higher than average percentage of married couples: Elk River = 61%, Minnesota = 54.15%, national = 51.2%. Elk River is also distinctly white at 97.2% versus 89.4% for the state and 75.1% nationally. This mirrors the ethnic ancestry of German (34%), Norwegian (13%), Irish (10%) and Swedish (8%).

Compared to other parts of Minnesota and the nation, the people of Elk River like to stay put; 79.3% were born in Minnesota compared to the overall state average of 70.2% and the national average of 60% for people born in the same state in which they currently live.

Elk River, with a current population over 18,700, is starting to work to rebuild its small town roots and its connection to the Mississippi River in spite of its accelerated growth driven by its highway location.

Outside Kemper Drugs, oil on canvas, 16" x 20", plein air

Rose Ann Ames
Age: 61 1/2
Interviewed in the Cub Foods parking lot
Elk River, Minnesota

August 20, 2005

Rose Ann Ames

Well, a little background. You were saying where you were born, where is that?

In Elk River, right in Elk River and it used to be a house where they, the ladies would go to have their babies. I don't know, remember exactly what they called it back then. But, it really wasn't a hospital. It was right on Main Street in Elk River. Across from, it was called the Car Nook, it was an old, there was a train car that was there and it was right across from the Car Nook. The Car Nook was called that and it was across the street from there.

A birthing center or something?

Yeah, right.

Where were your parents from?

My mother and my dad are from western Minnesota, Maynard, west of Willmar. That's where they originally came from. Then they came here to live in Elk River.

What brought them to Elk River?

I don't know, I think part of it was his brother had a restaurant in Elk River. They came here

and worked in the restaurant for a while then they stayed, just decided to stay in Elk River, I guess.

Do you have any other brothers and sisters?

Yes, I have two older brothers. One that lives up at Maryfield and my other brother, he lives in Meadowdale. So, three of us stayed around the area.

What was it like growing up in Elk River?

It was just a nice small town.

What was it like back then?

Well, we lived about two or three blocks from town and so we'd walk to town, you know, to buy groceries or do a few things. It was just a very nice small town atmosphere and now Elk River, everything was across the tracks on Main Street. And now, everything has come over, or a lot of businesses have come over now north of the tracks. So, it's changed that way and there's the high school and the grade school, like I said, I graduated from Hanke School in '61 and now it's gotten so much larger and that.

What were your first memories of the Mississippi River?

I don't know. We would just walk downtown and that. And the bridge, I guess, too, there's a dam that's west of Elk River. And we'd kind of walk out that way a little bit, but, I guess, we'd kind of stayed away, you know, there's a bridge here in Elk River, and because the traffic would go over it, you know, we wouldn't get real close to it or anything. And then the highway, Highway 10, was about a half a block from our house and I can always remember the trains and the railroad track was there, too, so I can remember the train going by and making a lot of noise and that.

Did you ever play or skate or do anything on the river? Boat or fish?

No, no, because right across the block from us was called the stadium next to the school. And that used to be, at one time there was a

lake or something there and they drained it out and then every year they would flood that and then kids could go skating there and we used to slide down, there was a hill there. You haven't been over there to see that, have you?

Next to the Hanke Center?

Yeah.

Yeah.

Yeah, yeah. Yeah, I just used to live right here (draws a map with her finger on the floor) is where the stadium is and then right across the Union Church here and there used to be a house right here on the corner, and that's where I used to live.

But my parents sold it to the Union Church and it was torn down and I got the old out house. It used to be a stage coach stop and it had a very big out house. I think it was a

Bagging the Goods

To Protect and Serve, oil on canvas, 24" x 36"

four or five seater and so when my parents tore the house down, I said, "I would like that." And we've had it on our property now for, I don't know, ten – fifteen years and it's kind of been coming apart and I asked my husband, I said, "Let's tear it apart. I want to take the 2 x 4s out" and we made some furniture out of it. So it has a meaning to me and the wood is over a hundred years old.

Wow. So, what did you do after high school?

I just stayed around here. I worked for an insurance company for five years and I had gotten married and we moved out to Nowthen, where we live, we've been out there for forty-one years. And I've been a housewife and I did work at a grocery store in Elk River. I worked at Ron's and did cake decorating, otherwise I didn't work out of the house too much.

And how did you meet your husband?

We went to a church and I met him at a church.

Well, looking back on what life was like in Elk River, when you were growing up, and what it's like now, what has changed the most?

Well, it's just grown so much. As a child, we thought it was fun just to, after it rained, we'd walk along the curb and where the water was flowing down, you know, the gutter or something like that, and it was just quiet and relaxing and now it's so much bigger and busier.

So, how has it grown?

Well, all the different stores and that. We only used to, we'd walk downtown to a store to get groceries as children and that. The post office used to be over there by the grocery store at one time and now, of course, that's moved. It's just that so much has moved north of the tracks and changed.

This used to be field. People, like I said, my brothers used to come out here deer hunting and squirrel hunting and that. So, it's just grown an awful lot.

Downtown's Secret

What has stayed the same?

Um, (pause) well, I don't live in Elk River, you know, so, I don't know, I guess maybe the Main Street of Elk River, that kind of, you know, some of the places there, there's the

bakery that used to be there when I was a child. You know, some of the stores. There's a few of them that have stayed there that are the same and that, but, what's really changed, too, is there is so much traffic going through Elk River. That's made it quite different and that.

And how far outside of Elk River do you live?

Eight miles. It's just in northwestern Anoka County.

Well, if you're looking forward like 20 years, what do you think this will look like? What will Elk River be like?

Well, it's just growing more with houses and new growth and grocery stores and lumber, you

know. Menards has come in and Home Depot has come in and so, in that sense, we don't have the small town hardware stores like we used to as much because we have the bigger building stores and that. And I guess that's what going to happen and then, of course, Wal Mart, you know, has come in too, so it's just developed a lot more where there used to be fields and farm land and it's the same out where I live, too. Used to be farm land but it's not that anymore, now somebody bought it and they're putting houses out there.

How many kids do you have?

I just have two daughters.

OK, do they live around in this area?

Well, the one daughter lives over by St. Francis and the other one lives in Virginia.

Well, what keeps you here?

Well, what kept me here is, I grew up here and then my parents lived here and, as they grew older, I helped to take care of them and, my husband's job, he came from Bemidji, and he came down here and then he got in Anoka, Federal Cartridge, and that, so that's the reason we stayed in the area. And, out where I live in the country now, I like it, and that.

OK. What would it take to have you move away?

Well, I don't want to move away.

Carting It Home, oil on canvas, 16" x 20", plein air

So, no plans to move?

No, no. I've been out there forty-one years and I don't want to move. My daughter with my grandchildren are around here and guess I was used to being around my parents and that and so I just like, you know, the closeness of that. Maybe some day we might move, but as of right now, we don't necessarily plan to move.

OK. Any last stories or connections or stories of the Mississippi or growing up here?

Well, like I said, it's just changed and grown so much, and the small town atmosphere, it isn't that much anymore. You have to kind of go out to western Minnesota. There are some, you know, smaller towns like that, to get into that. It's just growing so fast and, you know, more houses coming in and businesses and everything and that. I mean, it was just kind of nice to go downtown and, you know, go to the grocery store and now you have to come across the tracks to go to the grocery stores and a lot of places and that, so.

There was a creamery along the highway and over by the railroad tracks and, of course, they tore that down. It is no longer there. But, we went there to watch them make butter, because that's what they did. You know, where the farmers, where they brought the milk in and that, and some of the things in the train depot, they've taken that away, too, so, you know, some of those landmarks that you used to know of, they are no longer here.

Doug Johnson
Age: 57
State Farm Insurance Agent
Elk River, Minnesota

August 18, 2005

Where were you born, where did you grow up?

Elk River. I wasn't actually born here, but I've lived all my life.

What kind of schools?

I went K through 12 in Elk River, graduated in 1965. Then I did undergraduate work at Saint Cloud and graduate work at Mankato.

Where are your parents from?

Elk River.

Elk River, so you're at least second generation. How about grandparents?

Elk River. They both settled here.

Doug Johnson

How did they end up coming here?

Well, I think there were relatives that they learned of from the old country and associations and that matter, and that's how they ended up in this neck of the woods.

Well, growing up, what were your memories of the Mississippi River and Elk River? What was it like as a kid in Elk River?

Mayberry. (laughs) It was, in every respect. It was Mayberry. And the river, well, the beauty of the river and the recreational offerings of the river were integral in our lives.

What kind of things did you do?

Fish, just spend time walking up and down the banks, floating the river. Just appreciating the beauty of it.

Do you have any brothers or sisters?

I have five sisters, no brothers.

Are any of them still here in town?

Let's see, two of them still live in town.

What was high school like, kind of getting out on your own here in Elk River?

Well, it was just, it was just a sleepy little town. I mean, it was, it was simply the town where everyone knew everyone else and everyone knew everyone else's business and it was a very comfortable place to live and to be raised as a

child because it literally was the community raised the children because everyone knew everyone. If you went downtown and smarted off to someone, before you got home, your mother knew about it. And so, you had that to deal with. But, it was just a wonderful place to grow up in those days.

What was your first job?

At the age of twelve I started washing dishes in a greasy-spoon restaurant in downtown Elk River. Worked there all the way through my summers of my undergraduate college years.

What's your degree in?

I have an undergraduate degree in speech and a graduate degree in communication.

You said that Elk River has a very active arts community, what does "art" mean to you?

Well, it means quality of life. It means escape. It just means a fulfillment, a rounding out of the stresses of daily life and just putting a shine on our town, our state, our way.

Do you know any artists?

Well, I was involved in, I'm not an artist, well somewhat I guess because I was involved in, my emphasis as an undergraduate was in theater and then I was involved in starting the Elk River Community Theater, myself, and three other persons, in 1976. And I still, just as recently as last winter, directed a show for the Elk River Community Theater. So, I've been involved in that regard. I spent a little time in other media, but not very successfully, just for enjoyment.

What kind of things do you dabble in?

I like to draw, I like to paint, things like that.

Well, looking back to when you were growing up in Elk River, compared to what it's like now, what has changed the most?

It's become a suburban community in every respect. It's lost that sleepy-town feel in most regards. But, it remains too, it has held some of that flavor and some of us are doing what we can to continue that because I think that's one of the essences of the community, the uniqueness of the community, one of the drawing cards, one of the things we can offer.

In Case of Fire...

And, I hope we can continue, even as we grow, to maintain at least a degree of that.

Speaking in terms of the arts, it's just a quantum leap from what it was when we were kids. There were no avenues, really, for the arts in the schools or in the community. Now, it's beginning to blossom in those areas. It's always a struggle because the emphasis continues to be in other areas but, it's starting to blossom and I hope that our future holds more opportunity for the arts and for artists and appreciation of their work.

OK, I see pictures of family, are you married?

I am.

How did you meet your wife?

Through mutual friends and friends that I met and nurtured through the community theater, interestingly enough. So many, we joke about this all the time, so many of the core group of persons that started the community theater, were involved in the early days, met their spouses through the growing circle of friendships with that group. So, I guess I would have to say that's how we really got together, too.

And you have kids?

We have two children. We have two daughters, both of whom were involved in community theater. Both of whom still have a real keen interest in the arts. One more than the other. But, both still. One still performs, still takes dance lessons, teaches dance, and so her avocation is certainly the arts.

And where do they live?

One lives in Chaska. She's the oldest and the one that spends the most time with the arts. The youngest one continues to be a student and she lives in Denver, Colorado.

Well, if you're thinking what the town was like when you were growing up and what it's become now, and there have been a lot of changes, I see you have a whole commerce section that probably wasn't here twenty years ago, what's the town going to be like twenty years from now?

That's a good question, a little frightening. I envision the growth to continue extremely

dramatic, exponential. I don't think there's any reason to think it's going to be anything other than that. I hope that as that happens, the sense of community continues, is nurtured and grows. I hope we end up, someday soon, having like an arts center. Hopefully, we'll be able to do some of those things along the way.

Finally, the high school saw fit to have a theater included in their complex. And that was a long time in coming. Turned down many, many times, But, now we have that facility, beautiful facility. So, I'm just hoping that those things can prosper as we grow.

What changes have the Wal-Mart, Target, Home Depot brought?

Well, it's created in the community a sense of kind of business center or commerce focal point. I guess Elk River always was that to some degree. Even when I was a kid Main Street was extremely vibrant. I mean, there were like three hardware stores, couple of clothing stores, I mean it wasn't large by any stretch, but it was a vibrant kind of a commerce center.

And I think in the 21st century kind of feeling, it continues to be a commerce center with the big box retailers now. But, that's obviously just a totally different sort of persona because it isn't your neighbor that owns it and he and his wife that run it, back like it was like when we were kids. But, I guess that's the way we got to go.

What keeps you here in Elk River?

Well, I like it. It's a, I'm the second generation in this business. Between my father and I, we have almost eighty years of service to the community in this business. So, my roots are very deep. And, I don't like all the change. I think back fondly on my memories of by-gone days and how it used to be, but I recognize that it can't be that way anymore. But, in terms of putting my business hat on, I couldn't be in a better location for business. So, it's very good in that regard. So, we try to keep a bit of that small town flavor, like I said before, but then prosper in the advantages that the growth has brought to the business.

What would it take to get you to move away?

I suppose that if it lost, totally lost that sense of community that we fight to maintain. If it no longer offered the citizenry some of these things that we're working to establish, then I guess I would not be very pleased with staying on here. It would, the transition would have been so then profound and complete that it just wouldn't have any of the old appeal to me anymore.

Any other thoughts or observations, things you'd like to share?

Oh boy. Not that I can really think of off the top of my head.

I can remember as elementary kids, we would, a group of boys that I, everyone just kind of hung out together because there just weren't

Support Your Local Team

that many of us and we all played ball and we all would often times, particularly in the spring of the year, go down to the banks of the river, just probably four blocks from where we sit, slide down the banks and wade across the river. Go out to the islands, heat up a can of chili, fish and build a fort and that was a good part of life as a kid growing up here.

Either doing that on the islands on the river just a few blocks from where we are or on what we always referred to in Elk River as the "top of the world", which is now a development about six, seven blocks from where we sit. It's just an incredible spot. You can see downtown Minneapolis on a clear afternoon. I guess it's the highest point in the county. We always referred

to it as kids as the top of the world and we'd go up there and play cowboys and Indians and camp out and chase squirrels.

How old were you?

Oh, I would have done that from, well, in those days, you know, parents didn't worry about kids and so we would, just really from the time you could ride a bike, so I would guess probably the second or third grade and we continued to do those sorts of things until we became more involved in organized things, so probably until eighth or ninth grade. And that was just a big part of recreation. Just creating fun times in those environments.

Betty Thomas
Age: 58
Kemper Drug Store employee
Elk River, Minnesota

August 19, 2005

Give me a little background on where you were born, where you grew up?

I was born, actually, in the Monticello Hospital. My parents lived in Clear Lake at the time and my dad worked on the farm. They lived in a little house on a farm and he, my father worked for them. And then, my next recollection is coming to Elk River, right between Big Lake and Elk River actually. I grew up in the house where I am still living. Been there since I was five years old. Didn't get very far did I? (laughs)

That's not a bad thing.

And, it's right on the border of Elk River and Big Lake, like I said. The first two years of my life I went to Big Lake school because my sister and I caught the Big Lake bus. And then the Elk River principal came out and said, "Your girls are going to the wrong school. They're in the Elk River district, school district." So, we had to change schools even though we lived in the same house. The road was actually the dividing line, so we changed and went to Elk River. Graduated from Elk River. My husband did, too. I'm really a small town girl. Haven't gotten out of it very much.

Betty Thomas

So, as a young girl, what were your memories of the Mississippi River?

OK. My memories of the Mississippi River, the house we lived in there was probably half a mile maybe from the river. And back then, of course, it was very country. Had the dirt road and my relatives and neighbors were great friends, of course, and didn't live that close but we would get together and we would walk down to the river and we would swim. I started out swimming quite young. The rest were a little older. It was sometimes a little scary because you'd get caught in the current trying to get across to the sand bar, or whatever, you know, so one of the older

ones would come and help me, grab me.

We also skated on it in the winter time, too. I was probably about twelve when I went through the river ice skating.

Oh, through the ice?

And it was awful. It was terrible. I thought I was going to die.

How much of you went in?

Just up to my waist. Because, what happened was, I skated close to a tree that was coming down, and laying across the shore, across the river there. I mean, into the river there. And, I got too close to that, and of course, when the river hits something like the trunk of a tree, like that, that's laying across it, it thins the ice. And so, I just kind of skated too close, the ice got thin and I went down but I was able to grab on to that trunk of the tree that was laying there. So, I only went up to my waist and my sister and her, and the neighbor guy got me out.

But, it was like instant freeze. Oh, my gosh, it was horrible. I mean, it was like, get to the car, strip and get home as soon as you can. It was really, I'll never forget how cold that was.

So, there were people right there that saw you go through?

Oh yeah. I was with my sister and the older neighbor guy, friend of hers. And they could drive. They were four years older than me.

So, swimming and ice skating.

Did you ever do any fishing, boating?

I never did any fishing and we never owned a boat. My husband, on the other hand, was a town kid, and he went up the river every day. He lived on Lake Boreno, which the Elk River runs into Lake Boreno. And so, he had a row boat, I mean a, yeah, row boat but he had a little, whatever, ten horsepower motor, whatever, on it and would go up-river every day in the summer time. He said he'd go see how far up the river he could get with that little row boat before he'd get stuck, you know, have to turn back. Because he could just go across Lake Boreno and up the Elk River.

Do you have any brothers or sisters?

Uhm, I have one sister, who is four years older. No brothers. My father died when I was young, twelve years old, in the house where I still live.

Is the family still in Elk River?

His family's in Elk River. My sister is in Elk River. Still lives on the river. Actually lives on the Elk River, not the Mississippi, but just down the road from me. So, we're still in the same neighborhood. My sister and I both. Our parents moved, my mother and step-father moved up north to Hackensack. So that's how I ended living in the home place because my husband and I bought it when they moved up north.

So, how did you meet your husband?

High school. Well, actually, he was a grade ahead of me, but I didn't know him in high school. I came home, my step dad was in the army, so I had to go with my mother, of course, and so I was gone for a couple of years and I came home one summer to visit my sister and her husband was in a band with my, what ended to be my husband, he was a cousin of my sister's husband. So, I met him through my sister and her husband because he was in a country band with them. He's a musician. That's how we met. But, we did go to the same school.

After high school, what did you do?

I actually just started working here at Kemper Drug and I've worked here for forty years.

Forty years.

Yep. Just in February, it was forty years.

Congratulations.

Like I said, I just stay where I'm put, don't I? (laughs)

Well there must be good reasons for that.

It's strange. I don't know, I guess I'm satisfied with that, happy with that. My daughter on the other hand, she's a traveler. My son, he says to his sister, "Upper Big Lake and Monticello are big enough for me." So, he stayed right here. He built a house right next to us on our property.

So, he's still here.

So, he's got a home place.

Any other children?

No, just my son, I have a son and a daughter and five grandchildren.

And they're in Elk River?

I have three grandsons who live right next to me and two granddaughters that live in Omaha.

You had mentioned your husband was a musician?

Yes.

Taking a Break

Kind of in that vein, thinking of music and art, what does "art" mean to you?

Art means a lot to me. It means much more to my husband but, since we've been together all these years, you know, of course, you kind of think the same way. I think I was always a, we kid, he always says that I was a color-by-number person or paint-by-number. Which I was! When I was a kid, I loved that. I'd get those sets for Christmas and paint by number, you know. And then, after I married him, of course, he has to be all original.

He has opened my eyes so much to the art world. I treasure it. Right now, I think this country is really hurting because it hasn't valued the arts like it should. We've gotten so much into a sports culture instead of the arts and I think that hurts society as a whole.

Our most recent thing, well, it's been like

twelve years now, but my husband and I got into swing dancing. When our kids grew up, it was like, "We're getting older, the kids are gone. We need to find something we can both do and love." Well, since we loved music so much, and we were in a band together in our early years, and then he played in rock bands, and then we've been into blue grass, everything. The next step, of course, was we went back and we found the big bands: Tommy Dorsey, Glenn Miller, the forties. And we started collecting that music. Well then, it just hit us, "We love this music and we know it so well, why don't we dance?" So, we started dancing and I think the arts are so great for young people.

I guess that we've been dancing for probably twelve years now. We go down to the Wabasha Street Caves in Saint Paul and they are the only place in the Twin Cities with a live band, which is the ultimate for us. We don't go out dancing and pay money to dance unless it's a live band. We've got tapes and records at home, you know.

So, all the young people come there. When they started getting into the swing scene, the only place they could go in the Twin Cities with a live band was the Wabasha Street Caves. He allowed them in there and we've been going, you know, and we've had everything from thirteen-year-olds on up to our age and older, and there has never been a problem in twelve years. They've never had the police there. There's never been anybody caught drinking

or stealing or anything.

And, they're just good, good kids that come to that and I just think, "The arts are so good for kids." And especially one that they can get into where it's a multi-age because then the generations, the ages, I think it's just so good where they gather together from thirteen years old on up to seventy or eighty years old. And, everybody respects each other, loves each other, has the same passion for the music and the art that there's just, I don't know, everybody's just wonderful and gets along great. I think art does that for people.

Probably other things do too. When you have the same passion as other people it seems to really draw you in, of course.

Are you still a musician?

I don't, nope. I'm a dancer.

You're a dancer. You've transformed.

Yes, so much of a dancer that my husband and I built, we have our own outside dance floor. Like other people have tennis courts, we have an outside dance floor. It's just beautiful. Lit up, it's like a movie set. We were just out there last night instead of going down to the Caves because of the price of gas, we just decided to stay home and dance on our gorgeous dance floor with the full moon.

Sounds great.

Yeah it's fun, it's really fun.

Thinking back to what Elk River and the river was like when you were a kid versus what it is now, what has changed the most? That could be from a people standpoint or a town.

From a people standpoint, I see the biggest change as being so, the river is so built up. People own houses and own property along the river. You can't just go down there and send your kids down there with their tubes and let them go. You know, it's more like, you don't feel like you have access to the river as much as like when we were young. It was like *easy* access, you know. Now you're probably going through somebody's property or have to get permission. Can't find inner tubes like, man, did we have inner tubes. And then it got harder and harder and harder to find the inner tubes for floating down the river and that was always great.

So, I don't think people use it as much, you know. If you don't live on the river I don't think you really get to use it as much except for maybe fishing. Some people probably know where to go fish but, we don't really utilize the river fishing, just canoeing and tubing and skating.

How about the town of Elk River?

The town of Elk River, unfortunately, just doesn't use the river. It's been an issue for years where the old downtown, where I work, would love to utilize the river and make walking paths, bike paths down there. A park where people could gather and have concerts and different things. And, it just doesn't seem to pass. It's really, really sad.

The one park that they have, just a little ways out of town, Babcock Park, no one uses that, a few fishermen, but it's not a good place to go with a family, you know. So, I don't know if the downtown business people will ever get

this town to do what they've talked about for many years.

We have a group called River's Edge and they have proposed so many different things and they say they're going to do it, but they're going to do it after they tear that building down and they build a three story building across from us. So they're tearing down old buildings, putting up new buildings instead of really putting more time and funds into fixing up the river banks and river area that we could utilize because we had a building burn down over there so there is a vacant lot. And they were always going to make that into the park that goes down for an amphitheater and then

The Old Feed Mill

have all the walkways and the dock for fishing and all that down in that area.

Right here off of Main Street?

Yeah, there's been talk for years and years and years. The downtown development thing, you know, they just, I don't think they see it as a priority. Where other towns will see their river as just such a priority for bringing people in. This town doesn't.

What has kind of stayed the same, from when you were growing up until now?

I don't know if anything has stayed the same. (laughs) Except maybe me and my little parcel of land.

Are there many other friends, your childhood friends that are still here?

Yeah, quite a few. There's quite a few. And there are still kids that I graduated with that still live here. And it's nice since I work out in the public, that I do get to see people like that and see a lot of the old-timers. The original, you know. Like we just lost like three or four, what do you call it, that have been here forever. They just grew up here and, I mean you've known them your whole life, whether they were business men or just people that raised their family here and you went to school with their kids. But the town has grown so much that there's fewer and fewer. The natives are dying off.

And there's just fewer and fewer people that you remember from your childhood. It's sad. But it's nice having worked out in the public, like this all these years, that you keep in touch with them. So many of them do still come down to the old downtown for shopping, for their prescriptions, for whatever they can. Because I'm sure they have a place in their heart for it, too, the old downtown by the river.

Well, if you're thinking twenty years out, with all the changes that have happened in Elk River, what do you think Elk River will look like twenty years from now?

I think the biggest changes will be that there will be more two and three story buildings downtown with apartment space in the upper part. It'll pretty much, I don't think that we're going to see much growth as far as businesses down here. It's more services like lawyers and accountants, that kind of thing, you know, instead of businesses. I really think all the businesses will be pretty much on the outskirts like it is in so many of the little towns.

So, how has having a Target and a Wal-Mart and a big Cub affected Kemper Drug?

You know what? It's shocking, it has affected us, we've really gone down as far as your health and beauty aids, some over-the-counter items. But as far as prescriptions, it's amazing how many people still come here and how many prescriptions they do a day here. And I think it's because they still have that personal, one-on-one service. They can talk freely with their pharmacist, the pharmacist, you know, on duty, without thinking that there's a line of people waiting.

The owners here have so many, I mean, where other places might have, it might be a big place like Target or something, but they seem to really skimp on employees. They'll have a pharmacist and one or two helpers, where here, they put a lot of money into payroll, and they might have three other people in the pharmacy, sometimes four. And that does free him as far as being able to counsel people. And people really seem to like that, especially the aging population.

And with the insurance plans, and now and stuff, that you're going to pay the same price no matter where you go probably. Maybe even get a better deal here because we do offer senior discounts. And so, as far as like the health and beauty, you can get those probably cheaper. Every grocery store, besides the Targets and Wal-Marts, every grocery store carries them, and so that has slowed down. But then we've gone more into the gift line. And that's good because we have gifts that the others, those places don't. Real unique things and we're hearing that every day. When people come in here, they just go on about what great stuff we have.

What keeps you here in Elk River? Why have you never moved?

Roots! Parents and in-laws, you know. Your aging parents, you just can't leave and then, all of a sudden, I mean you're here because you grew up here. And then you have kids. And your kids are here so that they can know their grandparents. Then your parents are aging and they need you. And then all of a sudden you have grand kids, and if they stay here, you're not going to leave. So, it's like, we hate the winters, my husband and I both, and yet just that family, that family unit, it's just so strong that if your grand kids stay here, your kids and your grand kids, then you're going to stay here, too. Well, maybe we can get out for the winter, or something, but I don't think we'll even do that.

My daughter, even just she feels such a tie, she comes home once a month with her girls because she wants those kids to know her grandparents and their great-grandparents before they're gone. Just that little family feeling, you know, the roots are strong. It's a comfort to being familiar with things.

There's no plans to move?

There's no plans for me to move. I don't even plan on moving out of the house. I'm just so attached seeing as how I grew up there, my father died there. The trees I have were planted by him. I see the world through TV and movies. We did go to Hawaii for two weeks and that was paradise.

Any other thoughts about life here or Elk River?

You know what? A thought that just came to me was that my grandchildren are, the boys that live right next to me, are two, four and eight and we have yet to ever have them in the river. They've never been in the river! You know, isn't that odd? It's one of those things, where I say again, I can't just walk down to the old place where we used to go because there's houses down there now.

Just like we used to cross country ski down by the river. We'd go right out our back door and go down by the river and ski for an hour, you know, and come back. It was great! And then a few years, well I suppose it's been probably twenty years ago now, they put fifty-two houses along that trail where we used to go. You can't just do it. Ski out the back yard. It's not any fun anyway because it's not wilderness anymore. So, it's odd, I don't remember taking the boys down to the river. You know, we go to the cabin, the cabin up north. We go to the lake. We go to the beaches, other lake shore beaches, but not the river. So, I'm really not familiar with the river of today at all.

Mill City Morning, oil on canvas, 24" x 36"
Collection of Thomas and Katherine Miller

Minneapolis, Minnesota

Minneapolis, the largest city in Minnesota and the county seat of Hennepin County, has 382,618 people living within its 55 square miles. Together with Saint Paul, the two cities form the core of the 3,000,000 strong Twin Cities area. In addition to its Mississippi River connections, it encompasses ten lakes giving it the nickname, "City of Lakes."

Father Louis Hennepin was the first European to explore the area and named the only falls on the Mississippi River Saint Anthony. In the early 1800s, Fort Snelling spurred growth in the area leading to the first lumber mill in 1822. By 1840, the settlement of St. Anthony was growing on the northeast banks by the falls. Meanwhile, Minneapolis sprang up on the southwest bank and was incorporated in 1856. Quickly growing to city status by 1867, it merged with St. Anthony in 1872.

In 1883 the Park Board was established "to secure the necessary land for a grand system of Parks and Boulevards" and thirty acres of Loring Park were purchased for $4,904.00 per acre. Theodore Wirth, superintendent of Parks from 1905 to 1935, took the lead to develop and expand the park system. Dredging the lakes and grading their banks, Wirth removed the swamp sections and stopped the flooding.

He built a system highlighting the individual character of each lake: Lake Harriet with its family focused band shell, Lake Calhoun, sleeker and faster for volley ball and hanging out, and Lake of the Isles, contemplative

and perfect for canoeing. Now the 53-mile Grand Rounds parkway system connects parks, lakes, creeks, the Mississippi River and the 53-foot high Minnehaha Falls, made famous by Henry Wadsworth Longfellow in his "Song of Hiawatha."

While the park system grew, the economy moved from trading to lumber including some magnificent log jams at the falls. But processing the Great Plains' grain soon changed the focus of the city. Known as the "Mill City", with companies like General Mills and Pillsbury, it was the leading producer of grain in the world until 1932. In fact, the most recognizable woman in the 1940s after Eleanor Roosevelt was Minneapolis' fictitious Betty Crocker.

After World War II, Minneapolis continued to grow and by 1950 reached a peak population of 521,718. But soon that trend reversed as people moved out of the city to the suburbs. In the 1950s and 1960s, Minneapolis went through a major "urban renewal" tearing down 200 buildings; about 40% of the downtown area. "Skid Row" was gone and the Nicollet Mall was built to try to revitalize downtown.

Now there is a return to living in downtown. The last five years have brought over 9,000 new residents to the downtown core. New condominiums and converted warehouses focus on river views and with the Stone Arch Bridge and Grand Rounds River Roads, access to the Mississippi River is easy and enjoyable.

Granite and Glass, oil on canvas, 36" x 60"

Beverly Delores Cottman
Age: 62
Retired public high school biology teacher
Minneapolis, Minnesota

November 28, 2005

Tell me your name and where you were born, and a little background on yourself.

All right. I am Beverly Delores Cottman, and I live in Minneapolis, live in north Minneapolis. Now uhm, we've lived here a long time. We've lived here thirty-eight years. But I was born in Berkeley, California, and uh, but did not stay there very long. We stayed there till maybe, I was about two years old. And then my mom moved to Kansas City, Missouri, which is where I was raised – in Kansas City. Uhm, I stayed there all of my young life until I went to uh, graduate school in Washington, D. C. at Howard University. And that's where I met Bill. And then we came here in 1967, and we've been here ever since.

Beverly Cottman

So, was your mom, were your parents Californian?

No, as a matter of fact, my mom, uhm, was uhm, was born in Kansas City. And so, and then in her…sometime in her life, moved to California, and then uh, that's, so that's where I was born. But I grew up in Kansas City. That's where I went to school and, I then I, I went to college in a small college in Missouri. So kind of stayed in the Midwest, and now I'm back in the Midwest.

Well, growing up, what were your first jobs like?

Uhm…growing up…first job…babysitting. Uhm, let's see, I think it's, I think that's all I ever did was baby sit until I went to college. And then in college I worked, all through my college I worked in the library. And uhm, and then in summer I worked for either the NAACP or the Urban League in Kansas City in the summertime. So, kind of babysitting…library work, kind of office…filing, that kind of stuff. That's kind of my first work experiences.

Do you have brothers or sisters?

I have no brothers, no sisters.

You're the apple of your mom's eye?

Oh, yeah!

The center of the universe…

Yes, yes! But in uh, in Kansas City I was uh, raised with, with some cousins. So I have

Aquatennial Tennis

four cousins that are sort of like brothers and sisters. One girl cousin and three boys.

So, how did you meet Bill?

Oh, uhm, a mutual friend introduced us – a friend of his that he was uh, uhm living with in a house in Washington, D.C. was a school classmate of mine in, uh, in undergrad. And so, he, Kenny, knew Bill as his roommate and friend. But he knew me, you know, as a, as a hometown girl, and so he introduced the two of us. We, we were introduced by a mutual friend.

How did you end up coming to Minneapolis?

Uh, when Bill finished his degree in engineering at Howard, he got a job offer with uh, Univac. And so, he took the job offer and we got married on a…I think we got

married on a Saturday, and we moved here like on…Monday. (laughs)

Did you know anybody here?

No. We didn't know anybody. It was just us. Just us.

When was this?

This was in 1967, in June, 1967.

You came at an interesting time, too.

Uhm-hmm. Uhm-hmm.

What are your first memories of the Mississippi River?

Oh, well, that it was here, you know, and that it's, it's at its beginning, you know, what's way up further north than what we were.

Petitioning Dinkytown, oil on canvas, 16" x 20", plein air

Uhm. And I think just the fact that we lived in St. Paul when we first came here. So, there was another city on the other side of the river, basically. And I think we have always kind of gone back and forth. You know, whatever it is you wanted to do in Minneapolis – you did it. Whatever you wanted to do in St. Paul, you did it in St. Paul. Even though I know there's lots of people who stay on one side of the river. (laughs)

So, I think that was kind of our first…my first, kind of like saying, "Okay, here's this city that sits on a river, and there's another city on the other side of it. And, it starts in this state. So, it's, it's kind of…you can see across pretty easy." Uhm. You hear about the muddy Mississippi, the mighty Mississippi, and here it's just kind of like river-like. And then, when you get an opportunity to go further south, and you go all the way down to New Orleans, you know, now it's wide…and it's flat…and it's muddy…and, so… here there's lots of bluffs and that, that kind of stuff. And then as you move down it gets a little flatter.

So, if you're looking back to when you first came to Minneapolis versus what it's like now, what has changed the most?

Ah, well, first of all, there's more people. There's more people. Certainly, uh, the population is definitely more diverse than certainly in uh, in '67. There, you know, probably was just a sprinkling of any kind of immigrant population. Uhm, the population of African-Americans was small, and, and

also, concentrated in various parts of the cities – both Minneapolis and St. Paul. And now, you know, African-Americans are all over both uh, both cities and the metropolitan area. And there's this large influx of people from, like, all over the world that have found this place to be home. Uhm, so, in thirty-eight years, that's been a big, big change.

So, do you think that is good?

Yeah…I, I, uhm, population, you know, large population, metropolitan area, you know, how big does the area want to be?

Beach Ball

And, I don't know, uh, the things that a large population brings, uhm, you know, maybe there's some down side to that, you know, with crowding and traffic jams and stuff life that. But, uhm…I would say mostly good, mostly good. Just people being able to find a place that they want to live. Live there. Interact with people who are like themselves, and also people who are very different from themselves. Uhm…, you know, it's good, I think, good.

Looking back those thirty-eight years, what has stayed the same?

Stayed the same… mmmmm…what has stayed the same? Well, relationships that have been established…well, people you'd meet…you'd met, like, right at the beginning. A lot of people that we met as soon as we got here. Some of those people have moved away, or we don't see them anymore, but there's a core of people that are still the same, that we've known ever since we got, got here. So that has, that has kind of stayed the same, the relationships that have stayed the same.

Uhm, you know, there's

something about Minneapolis and St. Paul community wise that I don't know that is in some other places that are this size. But it seems kind of…family like. Again, I, I think it's those relationships. There seem to be relationships that have been established within particular neighborhoods, or around a particular church, or, uh, some kind of social kind of thing that just, kind of just stays no matter what is going on. And so, I think that part has kind of stayed the same.

Now, when you think about the river, you know, the river stays the same, I mean, the river stays the same, like. But, the…, you know, now there's lots of, uh – especially in the Twin Cities area – there's lots of development along the river. People are talking about developing the river and the riverfront and how they sell condominiums and houses, and taking factories that were at one time considered a blight, so now turning them into very expensive places to live. (chuckles) So, so in some ways, like, the river stays the same, but what's happening on the banks of the river has…

I guess the way it's being used has kind of changed?

Uhm-hmmm. Yeah. Uhm-hmm, uhm-hmm. And so, but in,…now see, in thirty-eight years…like, the mills were gone and so, you know, it wasn't used for that, but it was just kind of like, "Okay, here's the river. The barges go up and down. And there's not…and nobody's paying much attention." And now,

High Noon, oil on canvas, 24" x 36"
Collection of Martin and Jennifer Lacey

I would say in the last twenty years, people have really started to kind of pay attention to the riverfront and using it as an asset in the city, you know, drawing... They've built some things along the river and then people will, you know, they'll put art fairs, they'll build condominiums, and they'll clean it up, and, and so even though it's not used for, for so much running flour mills and things like that.

Well, looking out about twenty years or so, what do you think is going to change in your neighborhood, or the river, or what do you foresee?

HMMM! Oh, I don't know what is going to change. What I hope changes is, uhm, a focus on like, I don't know, housing, residential areas, places where people live; being uhm, accessible to a broad range of people that, you know, we don't just kind of categorize people and say, "Okay, we need some low income housing, we need some upper scale things with...but that, that every kind of place has an opportunity for whoever wants to live there to be able to live there. To make the city really livable and available to, to almost, you know, to everybody without a whole lot of division. Uhm, and, and, I don't know, I think it's just maybe my, just kind of the way that I kind of feel about equality and access.

It's really nice, you know, for a neighborhood to be really fine, and, and have nice homes and all that kind of stuff. But, if the prices go

up, the prices go up, the prices go up; then it's like only rich people can live there? And then...and now, what are you going to do? What about the people who are not rich? So, that's kind of what I hope is, that the city, both cities, start to look at – kind of, what is the picture of where we want to be in twenty years or thirty years? What kind of place do we want to be? What kind of defines us? And then, what kinds of things do we have to do to get that, whatever that is?

Now I, I think there's probably a lot of people who, who won't agree with me, you know. They want...they'll come in and gentrify everything, you know, clean it all up and, and play like there's not that other element. But there is, you know, and so. So, I kind of, I kind of want that, kind of, for the city. I want the city to be really livable? Just, just, really kind of livable. And then people can live, like, all over the city. They could do all kinds of things. The people who don't live close to the river, you know, know that there's things at the river for them to do if they wanted to go there, that it isn't just for those people who live down there by it. Uhm, that whatever the goods and services are that are all over the city...that people think, "Okay, this is my city, and I don't have to just stay in one little place. I can live all over." So that's what I want, I want it to be livable.

Good ideas. Good vision.
So, what keeps you here in Minneapolis?

Hmmm. Well, my daughter was born here,

Bright and Sunny

and, and she still lives here and so, that's, that's one reason. Uhm, uh, both Bill and I are retired and so we spent our working lives here, and even though from time to time, as everybody says, "Oh, let's go someplace warm; let's move to a different place." But it's, it's comfortable. It's a, it is still a very livable city. Uhm, it's a good size. I mean, there's enough, there's enough metropolitan, cosmopolitan type, type stuff, I mean, there's art, there's music, there's all of that kind of uh, aesthetic kind of stuff going on. Uhm, and it's, you know, it, it's close enough. I mean, there's a –I don't particularly care for Northwest, but – I mean, you know, there's an airline hub here. You can, you can get pretty much anywhere you want to go from here. Uhm, it's clean. So, there's, you know, and here's, you know, there's friends and relationships that have been established that are here.

What would make you move away?

Not being able to shovel snow! (laughs) Not being able to get rid of the snow, you know? Uhm, and I, I think with coming of, of uh, you know, getting older, and age, it might be...just kind of taking care of, of yourself and your home place with six months of cold and snow and that kind of stuff. Uhm, I don't, but I don't know, you know, I don't know what would...I don't think anything has come up. Nothing has come up that said, "Okay, let's go to some other place." Now, for a long time, uh, for a while my mom lived in uh, in San Francisco, and we used to visit her out there and that seemed a nice place. And, I think, once, I took a trip down into, uh, New Mexico. That seemed like, and that seemed like a nice place. And then you take a trip to Seattle, and say, "Wow! That, that's

Seven Corners, oil on canvas, 16" x 20", plein air

a nice place." Uhm, you know, the east coast where 'everything is,' you know! . . .to New York. But no. . .nothing has come up that just kind of says, "Okay, we should think about moving someplace else."

Kind of off subject – we're going to think about art. What does art mean to you?

Uhm, art is a part of life. It's, uhm, uhm, an expression of either your own, or someone else's creativity, their ideas about life and about things. Art is uhm, is one of those uhm, elements of, you know, kind of human existence that I think is necessary. I think that expression of creativity, an appreciation of creativity in whatever form, it's really necessary to be, to be human, to have a human experience. It's. . . You've got to have food and you've got to have shelter, but you've also got to have art, you've got to have that expression of creativity, that expression of what's going on around you in a way that sort of speaks to your soul, as opposed to just, you know, just taking care of basic needs. And I think everybody, I, I, think everybody needs that. So art is, is important in that way. It allows that to happen. So, I think it's very, very important.

Any other thoughts or comments?

Mmmmm, no. I don't think so.

Well, thank you, Beverly. Thank you very much for your time.

Brother Michael Collins

Age: 68
President of DeLaSalle High School
Minneapolis, Minnesota

November 11, 2005

Brother, where were you born?

Minneapolis.

Can you tell me a little bit about growing up in Minneapolis?

My first address was 1051 Bryant Avenue North, Apt. 307, the projects on the Near North Side, and I, I tell students that story, too, because I have come from living in the projects, to attending this school, to discovering a direction in my life, and ultimately returning to this school as President.

My first education, or is this not a question yet?

No, that's fine.

My first education was at the Ascension School in North Minneapolis, and at that time there were two black students out of more than a thousand at the Ascension School. Today it's just the opposite. I just recently had a conversation with one of our white students who was from Ascension, and I said, "How many of the students are white at the Ascension?" And he said, "Oh, maybe five or six." And I said, "Well, it's come full circle from when I was a student there. But it continues to

Brother Michael Collins

be a feeder school for DeLaSalle, just as it was for me in my time.

Where were your parents from?

Uh, well. . .a picture of my mother there, uh, with her parents. Her mother's mother was from Ireland. Her father's mother was from the reservation in the Duluth area, and she was born in Duluth. My dad, whose family is over there. . .there's a family picture of the, the homestead, the old homestead in the 1800's in Hastings, Minnesota, which, uh, at that time, I understand, maybe had two black families, one of which was my, my grandmother's family. And so, I guess, when we talk about the Mississippi, we could include some of those roots, especially my dad's. So, both of my parents were native Minnesotans, which is somewhat unique for African-Americans.

I was named by Governor Ventura to the Commission on Black Minnesotans a while ago – a state agency that advises the

Governor around issues that relate to black Minnesotans. New people come to the Commission and they introduce themselves, and so on, and invariably – "Well, I moved here from Detroit," uh, or "I moved here from Chicago," or wherever. And then they look at me and I say, "Well, I'm a black Minnesotan!" (chuckling) I mean, I'm re-hee-hee-ally one, which is, you know, kind of interesting. And, somewhat the black experience in Minnesota is, uhm, for the most part, pretty contemporary. But for some of us it is much more historical and is much more indigenous to the state of Minnesota. I happen to be one of those people.

Do you have brothers and sisters?

I'm an only child.

And then, from Ascension School, you went to DeLaSalle, here?

I came to DeLaSalle, here, and as a column that Nick Coleman did a while ago, which really made reference to the field question, I found my calling, as it were. I, uh, I interacted with a lot of Brothers who, even though I didn't know it then, and they probably didn't know it, were for me, role models (a term that came along later). And, I was inspired to do what they were doing. And so, at the arrival of the age of 17, I hopped on a train and, and last May I celebrated my 50th anniversary of that event. So, I've been doing this for fifty years. And I suspect this is what I will continue to do.

Where did you go to be trained?

Well, initially, Brothers go to Glencoe, Missouri, which was called the novitiate, which is like boot camp for Brothers. Then after a summer and a year there, the uh, the program continued in Winona at St. Mary's where Brothers were student Brothers. And after completing my time at St. Mary's, assigning was the custom in those days. The Head Brother decided. You didn't really decide where you were going to go, and, ironically, he decided I was going to go to DeLaSalle which I had only left four years before. So, interestingly, I came back to DeLaSalle after everyone who had been here with me as a student had graduated.

I came back in the fall of '59, and the class that had been freshmen, graduated in the spring of '59, since I graduated in '55. But many of the teachers were still here. I lived with some Brothers who had been my teachers, and it, it was interesting that, uh, for some of them I was still Mike Collins. Four years in the life of a teacher isn't nearly as long as four years is in the life of a high school student, which is all the years. But I adjusted to that, and I, uh, began by teaching freshmen. And, and there was, uh, kind of a caste system, in, in, informally, that young Brothers fresh out of college would teach freshmen, and if they could succeed with freshmen...

Or, survive?

Get 'Em While They're Hot

Yeah, then they'd move on to sophomores. So, I, I taught freshmen for a couple of years, then I taught sophomores for a year. I taught juniors for a year. I taught seniors for a year, and then I was made Assistant Principle and Dean of Students at a time when there were nearly sixteen hundred boys, and I was like the sheriff only I didn't realize what an overwhelming responsibility I had taken on. But, again, I didn't choose that. We were assigned to whatever we did, and...and accepted that. Uhm. We have two Deans here, in a school of six hundred fifty, and we had one in a school of sixteen hundred. But I believe that the two, in 2005, are more challenged than I was, because I,

I came from an era where long hair was a serious deal, and we don't get around to hair anymore. That's not an issue for us.

You've got bigger problems.

There are some bigger problems. The fights... fights are with more than fists, and today... Just a lot of what we thought was a, a serious felony in the '60s has become at the very most, a petty misdemeanor in the year 2000, so... But I survived that, and it really didn't take much to survive it, because I believed I was on top of that. Uhm...and then I was assigned to be Principal in Fargo, North Dakota.

Before we leave Minnesota, here...what are your first memories of the Mississippi River?

Well, my first memories of the Mississippi had to be as a student at DeLaSalle, because DeLaSalle is on Nicollet Island, and as an island it's in the middle of the Mississippi. So...there were, there were two sign posts of DeLaSalle. One was behind the Grainbelt Beer sign, and it's on the river.

(Interruption)

We had just talked about your memories on the Mississippi River and you had mentioned...

(Interruption) Dylan! What's going on?

(Interruption)

We have a program here where...I guess I introduced it about twelve years ago. In the old days we used to have home room advisors, that whole kind of system. It went...it went away. So, what I introduced was what we call mentors and...every student has an adult member on the staff – it can be a staff member or a teacher – as their mentor, we say 'academic mentor.' We adjust the schedule from time to time to look at that.

(Interruption)

So, memories – memories of the river? Did you ever go down and do anything on the river?

I threw my books in the river.

Did you start that tradition?

(Laughs) Ah, yeah. Right! We don't have it any more, interestingly, but there was that tradition that the…when one was finally finished at DeLaSalle, throw all their books off the bridge into the river. Uh…Which… you know, we weren't, uh, as ecologically, uh, sensitive in those days. And plus, today, books are pretty expensive, and so…people are more inclined to sell them than to throw them off the bridge.

So, what was this area like in the '50's?

Well, it had, uh, fallen into significant decay. Uh, Nicollet Island as it, as it plays a role on the river…probably is representative of the phases of life along the river. There was a lot of business, as you probably know, along the river. And those businesses no longer function, for the most part. And people who lived on Nicollet Island – it was a very fashionable part of Minneapolis, to live on Nicollet Island. As time went on, by the '50's and '60's, it was unfashionable and businesses were in decay. Uh, and it wasn't really a desirable place to spend time.

In fact, when I was a young Brother here, and we would have dances and invite girls from the girls' schools – I was recently reminded, because I wasn't as aware of it – that their dads would drive them down here and drop them off at the school and come back after the dance and pick them up. They didn't want their daughters walking around this

area – of the river, if you will. We were, at a time, referred to as 'river rats' by our friends at Benilde, which we referred to as 'swamp rats.' And, and the very fact that for time immemorial we've been 'islanders' speaks to our location.

Today there is a revival again, and I can look out this window and, and see that logo there, the star logo of the old blanket factory that no longer exists. But, Joe Duffey, class of '67 has a corner loft there that sold for…in excess…in, in seven figures. So it has changed again, and there's this

Me and My Shadow

transformation around DeLaSalle, around Nicollet Island of, uh, this being a very desirable place to be. As you saw, when I showed those kids from Totino-Grace my office, I showed them the river, which is very much a part of our history. Our school logo – our school logo incorporates the river if you've seen our logo.

Oh, yes.

And, with the water, symbolic of the river, and so we, we identify ourselves quite a bit with the Mississippi.

So, the economy and lifestyle of people on the river has really changed, but what has stayed the same?

DeLaSalle. DeLaSalle is a constant, and interestingly, as we, we have conversations with our neighbors about expanding our footprint on the island, many of them jump up and down and say it is their responsibility to protect the history of Nicollet Island. And I…I ask the question, "Whose history?" We've been here for 105 years *in this place*. People have come and gone. Businesses have come and gone. Every imaginable entity has come and gone and DeLaSalle has stayed. DeLaSalle has stayed - I'd like to say, because we love the river, that would be, would be the main reason. But, we have stayed because this is the heart of the city. And it is symbolic for us that we are here to educate the young people in the city and its environs, and, and that has not changed.

The, the city has changed. The make up of the city has changed. And, whereas DeLaSalle initially was white Catholic ethnic, uh, and the, the ethnicity was the basis of diversity—Irish, Polish, German, or whatever. Now the diversity is more color coordinated. But, it is the city, and what's interesting is even though the area around the river has changed, the city has changed – DeLaSalle is constant in being here to provide an education for families, primarily from the city, but also from the environs – even as far as St. Paul. And I think that's somewhat significant that our commitment has always been to the city, not necessarily to Catholic

87

boys, which was the story at one time. Not necessarily to white girls, but to whoever makes up the city, and today the city is much more cosmopolitan. And so it's no surprise, so is DeLaSalle. DeLaSalle is the most diverse private high school in the state of Minnesota. Thirty-five percent of our students are students of color. Twenty percent of our students are students of faiths other than Catholic. Fifty percent of our students receive financial aid of some kind or another. It's diverse by any measure, uh, but so is the city.

Looking like twenty years out, you know, there have been a lot of changes in the last twenty years. What do you think the city and your relationship to it will be twenty years from now?

We'll be basically the same. The school will be here. The school's mission, which is primarily to working class and poor people, which is primarily what makes up the city, uh, will be here. And we'll be here to respond to whatever those changes are. There was a time when we would not have thought, for example, of the importance of adult role models of color as part of an educational experience in a school like this. Today more than ten percent of our staff are people of color. We have three African-Americans on our staff who have doctorates, for example. These would not have been considered *as* important at one time, as they are today.

Sand Castles

We believe that the entire community experience should reflect the diversity that this school enjoys. And, that would, that's different today than it might have been. I was not assigned here because the school was predominantly black, God knows. I was assigned here because the Head Brother decided he was going to send me here. But we, we...the way we adjust, if we adjust at all, is we adapt from the standpoint of who we welcome to this school, and that is determined by whatever changes occur within the city itself, because we're here to serve city kids, as we have for one hundred five years.

So, do you have any plans? What would it take to get you to move out of here or to go somewhere or do something else?

Well, death is an option! That would be a motivating factor (laughs)! Aside from that I, I'd say that the years I've been here are longer than the years I will be here. Uh, I...There are some goals that I have for DeLaSalle that would benefit more from my leadership than from a new leader who is unfamiliar with the story, and, more importantly, with whom people might be unfamiliar with connecting DeLaSalle to that person.

We fell into this field thing. (Editor's note: DeLaSalle has no athletic field and was promised in 1978 that it could expand into shared use park board land to build one) I think it's legitimate, but it wouldn't have

been my first priority. But it had to do with the juxtaposition of various factors, not the least of which, we thought we had the votes on the Minneapolis Parks & Recreation Board, but that's because we thought we only needed five. Then we discovered because of the nature of this particular project, it required a super majority, so we needed six. Well, we have six now on the commission, which is...

It's kind of interesting that this island is populated almost entirely by a group of liberal, democrat activists who know how to play the political game. In some ways we were naïve about it. This is all new to me. I never took a course in land acquisition. But it's interesting that we have discovered that they underestimated the, the power and the influence of DeLaSalle not the, necessarily the DeLaSalle of 2005, but DeLaSalle from 1900 to 2005. And the sixty-five people who live on the island who thought their...uh, they had more than quantitative strength, but qualitative strength, and even, arrogantly said to, uh, our, one of our administrators, "Do you know who we ARE? Do you know who you're dealing with?" I mean, it was a lot of arrogance. So, I think they've been shocked to find that DeLaSalle, our, our influence permeates many areas of Minneapolis life. And, and again, one of them said, "Well I thought Brother Michael would throw in the towel on this deal," when he found out how difficult this might be.

But now it does look like you do have the votes and you're actually going to get a full sized athletic field?

It, it, it looks more like we will than that we won't. And uh, I mean the meeting with the, the woman who sat in that chair, they've got more money than they can count. And we're already looking at that phase of this…how we're going to pay for it, so…

Kind of shifting the subject a little bit. When you think of art, what does that mean to you?

Ahh, when I think of art, I think of something, uh…a form, or an expression that lifts the spirit and makes people feel good. And it comes in various forms. I was looking at some of that… that you've done. It lifts my spirits. Art lifts my spirits, and it, and it can be that kind of form; it can be a movie where something very touching happens that grabs me emotionally; music and, and the response is similar. Regardless of the form, if it's good art, and that's relative, of course. If it is good art to me, because, you know, there are young people today who would say that rap is a good art form. Well, to me, it does…it does not speak to my spirit. But many other art forms, because of the beauty I see in them, calls from me a certain exhilaration, and uh, an emotion. Uh, and, like I say, it can… I don't know, I recently saw some movie, and I can't even remember except that the resolution spoke to me about the beauty of relationships. I got teary-eyed, so…that's what I respond to.

Not Biting Today

Any other final comments or thoughts?

I'm amazed, I'm amazed at the fact that after all these years, Ron Merchant can still sit and be patient with the fact that Brother's doing all sorts of stuff. Some things never change! I uh…people here tried to get Joe Soucheray and Pat Royce to come for some event and they kept getting, "No, no, no." And so they asked me if I would call them. Royce went to Hill, and his kid went to Cretin-Durham when I was principal there. So, anyway, I called him. He said, "Sure, I'll do it," he said, "I think DeLaSalle's really a funky little school," and like, blah, blah, blah, blah, blah. So when he got up and started speaking he told the story, "I kept getting these calls. I kept saying 'No, no, no, no.' Then Brother calls and immediately there's a flashback and I'm finding myself, 'Yes, Brother. Of course, Brother. Whatever you say, Brother'"…and he showed up.

There's a relationship that you and I have that uh, isn't necessarily explained, but it's a, a, constant, you know, we have a history, you and I…have a history. And a lot of those good times flash back as we talk about other things. And you cannot help but ask yourself, "Where did those years go? How could all of that have…how could he be a grandfather? Because, just yesterday we're down the hall coming in for chorus!" Where did it go?

And see, for me, the clock kind of stops and it kind of doesn't. Because, with my job here I encounter a lot of alums, and then I speak about them, and I use the word 'kids' because that's kind of locked in my memory where our story started. And since I haven't been with them every day since, it's still kind of…like I said to you, I see a sixteen year old even though he's not anymore. But we have that history, and I value that as I look at other things I might have done.

I go to some event sometimes and people see the DeLaSalle and they say, "Oh, do you have a kid at DeLaSalle?" and I say, "Well, yeah. Six hundred and fifty kids, and they go, "HUUUUHHHHHuhhhhh." But that relational thing is very LaSalle even though we didn't know it at the time. St. DeLaSalle, in his writings, says, "The greatest miracle you can perform, Brothers, is to touch the hearts of your students." And that's relational. And I look back, or even today…when I just talked to that kid and let him know that I'm aware there's something going on and I'll be around for that, no matter what that is.

I think DeLaSalle, three hundred some years ago was really a smart guy, even though we didn't necessarily realize how smart he was because we didn't stop and read what he wrote. But it's that sort of thing and I think it happens in what we used to call 'Brothers' schools,' where the hearts of students are touched in some way, and they are made to feel that they are valuable; that they are lovable. And being made to feel they are

Separate But Equal

lovable, they, they are free to be more loving to others. And why we don't sit down and analyze it, as I look back, and now as I look back at my career I think that when people say, "Well, what's different about this Catholic school?" Well, there's a philosophy that the Brothers have, and it's a, it is a horizontal relationship – brother, not father, you know. It's brother, and that's relational, and that's, that's horizontal, and there's a certain quality there. Well,. . .

Thank you for your time.

Frank Brooks Evans
Age: 85
Retired artist
Minneapolis, Minnesota

December 12, 2005

Frank, tell me a little background. Where were you born?

St. Paul – Cherokee Heights, St. Paul, Minnesota

What was it like growing up in St. Paul?

It was, uh, my father. . . you don't have to write all this down. My father was a writer, a newspaper man, and he was an alcoholic also. It's a long story, but he became an

alcoholic about the same time that I was born, due to the sleeping sickness which none of the doctors in the Twin Cities could diagnose. That was 1920. I'm just giving you this as background. He was a Dr. Jekyll and Mr. Hyde. He was a perfect gentleman when he was sober, but the devil when he was drunk.

Did you have brothers and sisters?

I had two older brothers and an older sister. The older sister. . .they're all dead now. I've lived longer than any of them.

And how old are you?

I'm 85. No, my sister died when she was, I think, 93. I'm 85 now, I just was. But she was 93, but for, I'd say, the last almost ten years

of her life, she had Alzheimer's, and the last, I'd say, 3 or 4 years, she didn't know anybody.

When you were growing up in St. Paul, how long did you stay in St. Paul?

I stayed there until, really until World War II. And uh, but I did other things in between. I came back to St. Paul.

So, what was it like as a kid growing up?

It was wonderful, from the standpoint of scenery and so on, because I was only about three blocks from the Mississippi riverbanks. And, and there was a brick yard, it was a wonderful place. And, also, we used to walk out to the tracks and pick wildflowers. It was very, very woodsy. And occasionally out there, we would meet uh, uh, bums. They had a, a regular camp there where they would stop, you know, and they'd chat with you. And that was interesting, but playing on the banks I learned to ski, you know, on the banks of the Mississippi. Had a pair of five foot skis. And so, it was great. Uh, and uh, we spent a lot of time on the banks of the, on these huge banks along the river. And uh, a very interesting place. We'd play down there. But I learned to play tennis there when I was about 12 years old. And we had tennis courts just a couple of blocks. So from that standpoint it was fine – middle class neighborhood. And, uh…

Where'd you go to school?

Uh, Humboldt High School or, or Douglas School… Humboldt High School.

And that's a public school?

Yeah. (chuckles) And I was jock. I was on the track team, and the swimming team, and, and the uh, we called it, the tumbling team in high school. So, I was kind of a jock. I could run like, I could run like a…I'm just telling you, you don't have to write this down. I could run like a…I was the fastest guy every place I went. But I weighed 112 pounds and I was the same height that I am now, 5' 8 1/2", in high school. I never grew after high school. And uh, so I, I wanted to go out for the football team, but my mother didn't want me to. She was afraid I'd get hurt. Ah, but I would play scrub football.

Frank Brooks Evans

And I broke my wrist but never had it set, because I was afraid to tell my mother I'd been playing football. Uh, so that, that's been a hindrance in tennis.

What kind of job did you have?

Well, uh…

Did you work during high school?

Yeah, well, I've had menial jobs. When I was very young I shoveled walks, cut grass. Uh, later – caddied. I was a caddy at Summerset Country Club where I could play golf once a week. And uh, met up with some millionaires who were very wealthy fellows. And that was a long walk away, but I would walk up there during the summer to caddy. And uh, I worked one summer, how old was I? About 18, I think. I worked at a summer resort up in northern Minnesota. And did everything that a guy has to do to at a summer resort. Uh, my father taught

me to hunt and fish, and so I would take guys out fishing. That was my summer job.

After high school did you go on for other education?

After high school I went to…I got a scholarship to Macalester College, but in order to live…I was making my own living, my family had broken up…I was working in Hill Reference Library, uh, as a page. It was a wonderful place to work because I had the world at my fingertips – the books in the library. It was a reference library. And uh, I was a page for two years there. The first year, just a page.

But I came up with a way of finding books rapidly, in this library. And (chuckles) uh, the librarian said, "Frank, the head librarian wants to see you, Miss Starr".

"Uh-oh! What have I done wrong?"

"Well, you go in and see." So, I knocked on the door.

"Come in, Frank. Sit down, Frankie. You know I've been hearing a lot of good things about you. I want you to know that the things you do for the library are very much appreciated. Henceforth onward, your salary will no longer be 30¢ an hour. It will be 32¢ an hour!" (laughter) Well, and I'm living on that, I'm living on that! But, I'm living with my grandparents, after our family dissolved.

Where were you living then? Where were the grandparents?

Same place over in Cherokee Heights. Okay. Where are we now?

Well, did you finish school?

College? No. No, uh, one year. Then I got a scholarship to uh, the St. Paul School of Art – full scholarship to the St. Paul School of Art, with Mac LeSeuer, a well known name. And uh, while I was going to…uh, while I…Oh!…that was the St. Paul School of Art that was on Summit Avenue in those days. That's where I got my scholarship – the St. Paul School of Art. But no! No, that wasn't Mac Le Seuer, that was…I'm getting ahead of myself. That was uh, Cameron Booth, well known artist. He headed that. Uh, Mac LeSeuer; that was after World War II. But

Sneaking a Peek

anyway, uh, uh, I lived at the art school, and I had my own little apartment there. And uh, all I had to do was stoke the furnace. That's all, and then check the locks each night.

That was very interesting. A fellow named Wischki years later, uh, bought that place and said it was haunted. That was a big old mansion on Summit Avenue. Uh, I don't believe in haunting, that sort of thing, but I, at that time, I think maybe I did take it seriously. In an old place like that, there are a lot of strange shadows, and squeaks and groans. And it was a spooky place to live. But I loved it!

Did you finish your studies at St. Paul School of Art?

No. After I'd gone there for, I think about a year, World War II broke out. And uh, some friends of mine joined the Medical Corps down in Chicago, and uh, my mother, uh, didn't want me to go into the Army at all, but I said, "I'm going to volunteer, Mom. But I'll volunteer for the Medical Corps and that way I don't have to kill anybody." Well, she didn't like that either, but anyway, that's what I did. And I uh, so I was a medic during World War II.

Oh, and all this time I was always drawing. Or, painting, if I, if I had the materials.

And you're married now?

Ahhhh

Tell me a little bit about your family.

After World War II, uh, I had a friend who had a sister, and I, I met her after World War II. And uh, I came back and this friend. . .I had no place to live, really, except with relatives. So I lived for a while with my aunt, but just for a short time (aunt and uncle) in St. Paul. And uh, but then this friend of mine said, "Why don't you come over and live with us and go to Walker Art School?" It was within

The Lunch Wagon

walking distance. So I did, and eventually I married his sister. And uh, we lived in Minneapolis and had uh, uh. . .four children, three sons and a daughter.

Now, we're back from the war, aren't we? I landed on Omaha Beach, by the way. It

was D Day plus some months. The beach had been secured when I landed there but we had to wade to shore. And uh, during, during World War II, uh, I was, uh, we were in France for a while where we had a tent hospital, and uh, then we moved up to uh, Germany. And we ended up in the Hermann Goering Lüftwaffe which was a hospital named after Goering.

What did you do after the war?

After the war I came back and uh, that's when I got married, after the war. And uh, we lived in a rented apartment in Minneapolis, and I went to Walker Art School on the GI, on the GI Bill. Walker Art School. Graduated from there. And before I

graduated, they gave me a job teaching art. Uh, Mac, Mac done a lot with me. And uh, so I taught drawing and painting.

So, what does art mean to you?

What does art mean to me? Many things. Many kinds of art. But uh, my, my favorite kind of art. . .I did very well with the figure when I was in art school, but it never interested me nearly as much as landscape. And I ended up pretty much as a landscape painter.

Well, thinking back to the Mississippi River and the St. Paul area, what has changed the most from when you were growing up there to now?

The brick yards? It's no longer there. I mean the, the brick yards closed down shortly after World War II. It was one of my favorite places to go, one of my favorite places to play as a child. And uh, essentially that's what it was – brick yards. They made brick. And uh, there are clay banks on the, on the banks of the Mississippi.

This is on the St. Paul side?

Yeah, on the Cherokee Heights side.

Cherokee Heights side, okay.

Uh, what was the question again?

Well, what's changed the most?

Well, to begin with, after the war, huh! I moved to Minneapolis, which was when I was in high school, Minneapolis was that city, that progressive city across the river! So I moved clear across the river, and went to Walker Art School where I graduated. And uh, what had changed?

Oh, let's see, what… Uh, there was a lot of businesses located along the Mississippi River when I was a kid, especially uh, down, down the river from St. Paul a short way. And uh, well, right around St. Paul on both sides of the river. That's been turned into, it's all been put into parkland, and uh, it's uh, much nicer than it was when I was a kid. In that way, in that respect. But in other respects not so many good changes. And, of course, I didn't inhabit it, after World War II, as I had as a child. I really enjoyed it when I was a kid.

Well what good stories do you have about you on the river?

On the river? (chuckles) Don Koza, a friend of mine who eventually became a surgeon, he was my best friend, uh, for a time. Prior to that George Snell was my best friend. We used to go out rogueing. We made archery equipment. His father made archery equipment. He and I each made our own bows and arrows, and then we did a lot of shooting, and I, I was very good! I was very good. But, uh, what was the original question again?

Oh, just memories of adventures you had on the river.

Uh, one of the earliest adventures, uh, I was missing. The family went looking for me. They

eventually found me wading in the Mississippi River. I was about four years old, not in school. Wading in the Mississippi River down at Harriet Island. I'd gone down there with a, with a kid that was a little older than I was. (chuckles) That was quite an experience. My mother was, was beside herself.

And then, Don Koza and I – it was the spring

Well Girdered Bridge

breakup and we were in high school. And, I think we were in high school…anyway, spring breakup, and the ice was coming down the river and I said, "Wouldn't it be interesting if we got on a cake of ice and took her down the river!"

"W-e-l-l-l-l, I don't know…"

And I said, "Well, I'm goin' down. You wanna go with me?"

"OK."

So, a big cake of ice came down. We jumped on that cake of ice, and as soon as we did it started to tip…like that? And the first thing you know, the current took us out…the

shore out there, and we're out here, "Now, what do we do?"

And Don said, "How are we gonna get off this thing?"

And I said, "Don, I wasn't thinking about that!"

We could see about a block down, where

it looked like our cake of ice might come pretty close to the shore and there was a big tree, hanging over the tree. And I climbed up into that tree and I, and, I said, "Don, we have to, we have to get off here, because beyond here there is no getting off." So, I got, I scrambled up into that tree, grabbing branches – as I said, I was very athletic. I was a tumbler, what we called a tumbler, but uh, and, and then with my help pulling Don up any way I could, I got him into the tree and we scrambled to shore! (chuckles) That was very exciting.

Did your parents ever know about that adventure?

We never, we never told them, anyone about it. That was, ..so stupid! I wasn't even in high school, might have been in 8th grade, probably the 8th grade. What other adventures? Well, that was one of the main ones. Well, also I would go to…I was also a counsel…well not a counselor, but a, uh, I did dishes one year, and the next year was a…worked in the waterfront of YMCA camp on, on the St. Croix River down from Hudson, below Hudson. And uh, ah, that's where I learned to canoe and became a lifeguard.

Thinking back to the Mississippi, what has stayed the same since you were a kid to now?

Generally, I would, I would say things are pretty much the same as when I was a child. But more businesses and more residential people moved in across the river from me. Uh, when they had the, during the State Fair, I remember they'd have fireworks every night at the state fair and I could see them from the banks of the Mississippi. And Cherokee Park was one of my favorite places. It's primarily where I first learned to ski. And

How do you spell that?

Pickerel. Like the fish.

Okay, Pickerel, okay?

Pickerel Lake. And we used to dive off the trestle in uh, into, uh, Pickerel Lake. But uh,

Safe to Go

uh, then I became very good could ski these paths, and uh, I couldn't anymore. But I only, the skis were only 5 feet long. Uh, and as I say, the brick yards is gone, but I think the rest of it remains pretty much the same. And uh, uh, before the war I could go down, and I started a butterfly collection. And there are wonderful areas between or around Pickerel Lake, that's where I really learned to swim.

there was a train that went across, across the uh, lake. We'd climb on to the trestle and dive from there.(chuckle) Not a good idea, but we did it anyway. Had a lot of adventures there.

Well, if you're thinking into the future, you know you've seen some changes. A lot of things have stayed the same. What is Minneapolis, in relationship to the river, going to be like in twenty years?

From now? From now what's it going to be like?

In the future.

I think it will improve, continually improve, because they've found the river is a great resource. And uh, I think there will be more uh, uh, building of uh, homes, and uh, maybe restaurants and that sort of thing along the river. Uh, they're already doing it over in St. Paul, primarily, I think, and to, to some extent in Minneapolis. So... and the river is also being cleaned up. But there was a lot of sewage going into the river in the 1900s. And uh, I think it's going to continually improve for the general public. And Harriet Island has become quite a, quite a good spot to go to for various things.

And I went down there, they had a little zoo, so I loved that. All this time, by the way, I was drawing. Later on it was paint.

What keeps you here in Minneapolis?

I like Minneapolis very much. I like where we live, here. It's very nice. But for two years I went up and... I took two years off from work, and went up and lived in northern Wisconsin. Yeah, you might put that in. That was a very important thing.

Uh, I had read Walden, by Thoreau. Fell in love with his ideas. But I wanted a Walden of my own. That was the place he called his home, Thoreau. I wanted my own Walden, well I found it up in northern Minnesota; or, northern Wisconsin. And uh, I, we found it.

My wife and I found a wonderful place. And at the local, at the uh, at Woodruff they needed somebody who was very good, my *then* wife who was very good at banking — and she was! She was a banker. Eventually became the president of the bank. And they wanted her to move up there, and so we went up and took a look at it and I said, "This is great! Let's find a place to live." And uh, we did. We had a brand new modular home on a lovely lake, on Little Spider Lake, out on a peninsula. During the summer there were several hundred people around. During the winter, there was one family and us! Well, that's when I found what 'cultural isolation' meant. No good library. And uh, there was a small hospital there, but they were...it was uh, uh, uhm, not able to handle every kind of an illness or injury. And uh, I liked it very much.

But, one night, the first or the second year we were there, during the winter it was 40° below and our only neighbors who were about a block away on this peninsula, the only neighbors, they had come over. We were playing cards. The furnace went. A brand new furnace and I knew nothing about that. A water heater, a uh, baseboard water heater. That scared the hell out of me, and uh, because I was afraid.

everything would freeze up. I could not get anybody to come out. I lived seven miles from town, which, incidentally, was how far Thoreau lived from, from Walden, or uh, from his town, I forgot. And uh, but he could walk to town and his parents lived there. And he only stayed there for two years, I discovered after I got home. I felt bad, leaving after two years.

Prior to moving, or just before we moved, my car was demolished when a car run into us. I ended up in the hospital, not knowing who I was. That was here in Minneapolis. Uh, had to get a new car, of course. And uh, we, anyway, we moved up to northern Wisconsin. So, for the first year I was all. . .I had broken ribs, severe concussion, and uh, was not in good shape and I couldn't do very much, but, it was. . .I went fishing the first year in a canoe and uh, uh, fishing boat.

And I took my canoe out and uh, the first fish I caught was a muskie – it was about that long! But, he was skinny and I thought, "Well, if they're, if they're that easy to catch, I'll throw him back," and I did. And that was the last one I caught. Anyway, so uh, what else can I tell you? Well, I lived up there for two years and I became good friends with a fellow nearby who had a little resort. Uh, Harv Coleman. He and I spent a lot of time together fishing and so on. And uh, also I had a job there. I did some

drawings for a local uh, architect. Uh, well not only, he built houses and uh, buildings, and I did drawings for him. And my wife had this wonderful job at the bank. So, we were well off. And uh, I had saved up money to buy the house. So we could buy everything right off the bat. Uh, and that was a wonderful

Riding the Rail

experience. But, as I say, I felt very bad when I left, because I thought, I, I, I'm disgracing poor old Thoreau by leaving. But then later on I discovered that he only stayed at Walden for two years. So, I felt better about it then. But it was just 'cultural isolation.'

Now that you are back in Minneapolis, what would it take to have you move away from Minneapolis, do you think?

A great deal, because our families are located here or nearby. Both Barb and I, and uh, Barb Webb and I are 'living in sin.' You don't have to write that, but we've been together, I think, for about twenty-five years now. And uh, we're very happy together. After our miserable experiences with our first. . . She

was uh, married to uh, uh, an alcoholic and manic-depressive who. . .a very nice guy, again when he was sober, but, impossible when he was in a manic condition. In fact he used to go around. . .uh, he uh, on occasions had gone around the neighborhood stark naked preaching in the guise of Jesus Christ. That's how bad it was. It was so bad she finally had to get a divorce for the sake of the kids because it

was too embarrassing to them. My first wife, also, was uhhh. . .a very poor choice. I felt sorry for her. I got married because I felt sorry for her.

Any other thoughts or comments about the meaning of the river in your life? Or, the meaning of art in your life?

Yes. Uh, well, when I think of my early childhood and the things that I loved, I loved to go down to the river. I loved the view of the river from the Wabasha Street Bridge and from the High Bridge. And uh, much of my childhood, with much of my childhood, the river was very much involved. You know, it was quite a trek down to the river. I'd say that was a mile and a half, maybe two miles down to the river. Well, that's a. . . well, it depended on which part of the river I went to. So it was. . .and uh, we, we. . .boys had a wonderful time on the banks of it. Oh, we did all kinds of things.

Well, Frank, thank you very much. Thanks for your time.

Saint Paul, Minnesota

Just across the Mississippi River from Minneapolis lies Saint Paul, the capital and second largest city in the State of Minnesota. The smaller twin in the "Twin Cities", Saint Paul is known for its classic architecture and small town neighborhoods.

In the early 1800s, treaties with the Native Americans officially opened the area for settlers who lived near Fort Snelling along the confluence of the Mississippi and Minnesota rivers. However, settlers were soon banned from military property. One whiskey trader, Pierre "Pig's Eye" Parrant, moved down river and established a trading center known as Pig's Eye Landing. In 1841, the St. Paul Church was built and the name of the settlement was officially changed to Saint Paul. With continued growth, Saint Paul became a city in 1854 and when Minnesota was admitted to the union in 1858, Saint Paul became the 32nd state capital.

In the mid 1800s, Saint Paul was a busy steamboat port bringing settlers in by the hundreds. But, by 1870, the railroad had put an end to the dominance of riverboat traffic. Railroads were big business and James J. Hill rose from being a steamboat company bookkeeper to building the Great Northern Railroad and the Northern Pacific. He built a mansion of a home high on Summit Avenue where he could look back onto the Mississippi.

Summit Avenue leads to the St. Paul Cathedral and to the State Capitol building designed and built by Cass Gilbert. The current state capitol was completed in 1905.

Saint Paul took a different approach to renewal than Minneapolis did even though it had a similar exodus of people and business in the 1960s. It retained and restored its classic buildings. Now its downtown green spaces like Mears Park and Rice Park are surrounded by beautiful brick buildings that add to the charm.

Even though its buildings haven't changed, Saint Paul's people have. Saint Paul is now a racially and culturally mixed city with 67% white compared to 89.4% for the state. Its ethnic ancestry of German (22%), African American (12%), Irish (11%) and Hmong (9%) provide a diversity of cultural experiences for all. In fact, Saint Paul has the world's second largest urban Hmong population.

With a median household income of $38,774, well below the state average of $47,111, Saint Paul has its economic challenges. But there is a neighborhood for everyone. From the posh and stately Summit or Crocus Hill neighborhood to the transitional Frogtown area there are people tied to their roots and proud of their city.

Through its thoughtful riverfront renewal at Harriet Island, Saint Paul once again shows that it values and treasures its connection to the Mississippi.

Inga Weberg

Age: 55
Interviewed in Mears Park
Saint Paul, Minnesota

August 12, 2005

Okay, Inga, the tape is rollin'. Where were you born?

I was born here. Well, I was born in Minneapolis.

Did you grow up in Minneapolis?

Grew up in Minneapolis, the north side, and my parents were Swedish immigrants. And my father, uh, was a teamster and delivered milk to schools and hospitals. And always

Inga Weberg

told us how lucky he was, as a dumb Swede, to get such a good job and to get education.

Do you have other brothers and sisters?

I have an older sister. Sandra.

Is your family still around town?

My parents are gone. My sister lives in nearby Wisconsin.

Where were your parents from?

Vesteros, Sweden.

So, they actually immigrated.

Uhm-hm.

How do you spell Vesteros?

Let's see if I... I've seen about four spellings of it. On my mother's birth certificate it's , 'V E S T E R O S.' And then there's some kind of an umlaut thing, over the... something.

Where'd you go to school?

Uh, we lived in Minneapolis until I was about ten, and then we moved north to Brooklyn Center. I would like to say we were part of 'white flight'.

Did you go to public schools?

Public schools? Yes. They wanted me to go to a Christian School - Minnehaha Academy. But, they asked too late. I didn't want to go.

Brooklyn Center?

Uhm-hmm.

How long did you live there?

Well, the rest of high school, and then went to the University of Minnesota.

What did you study?

I studied music, and I was a music teacher in the public schools for several years, and then

A Quick Bite

left that and became a publisher's sales rep, and now I'm a marketer and sales manager for a publisher.

Well, that's pretty neat. What kind of music do you do?

Uh, primarily a pianist. Uhm, sang also, I was a choral director, so...and I gave piano lessons. Sang at weddings and funerals. Liked the funerals better.

Ever sing in a band?

I, matter of fact, one summer, my senior year, I filled in for...it was Barbara or Betty Simpson with the Barbara Simpson Trio. We did pop songs like 'Bad, Bad Leroy Brown', and did the Holiday Inn circuit around the Dakotas, and it was probably the worst three months of my life. Not only were we mediocre, but I discovered I didn't like starting work at nine at night and going until three in the morning. It was awful.

Tugs at Harriet Island, oil on canvas, 24" x 36"
Collection of Thomas and Katherine Miller

Yeah, it's tough.

Well, changing the subject a little bit, what does art mean to you?

What does art mean? Oh! Art is the soul, art is glory, art is the highest calling that human beings have. Art is what differentiates human beings from the cute little puppy dogs in the park. I mean it's, it's what gives us our spirit.

Other than music, do you do any visual arts?

No, I'm uh, quite retarded when it comes to the visual arts, so, I'm even more...I'm in awe of visual artists, crafts people, people who dance, anything that I can't do. I mean, we're all like that, aren't we. You know, we envy what we can't do.

Do you know any artists?

Uh, casually. You know, there are several that live in my building and around here.

Thinking back to when you were a kid growing up, what were your first memories of the Mississippi River?

The Mississippi. Well, I can remember that we went to Minnehaha Park, and Minnehaha Creek drains into the Mississippi, and my earliest memory is that my dad thought it was very funny, on the bridge going over the creek, to hold me out over it to scare me. And I remember seeing the water tumble down. And then, of course it goes into the

falls, but the river itself...let's see. We lived, probably about three miles from the river, and I couldn't go there until I was older. But, we would... Oh! Here's a memory – driving on bridges over the river and looking out when you're little, and that funny sound that the tires make going over those – remember those old bridges that had the steel grids?

That were open?

Yeah, and I remember that it was kind of scary, and the river was just huge. Seemed huge and dangerous.

Did you do anything with the, around the river when you were in high school?

High school, we were up north... Well, girls and guys would uh, kinda' sneak down along the river by campus and make out and stuff, have picnics, whatever. It was, once I was at the U it was even better, because we were down by the river playing frisbee, and people would bring their dogs.

When did you move to St. Paul?

In 1995.

Well, kind of thinking back to what the Twin Cities were when you were growing up, and what they are now, what has changed the most?

The most, uhmm...

What changes have you seen?

There are so many. I think...I hate to say the roadways, but I was listening to a documentary on MPR on the way home today, and they were talking about how just sixty years ago there were no freeways. There was no anything, and it's just...I remember when I was real small we took a streetcar. We had streetcars. Those were gone. And they ripped up all those beautiful brick streets, and replaced them with buses.

Before the Big Day

And the traffic. Uhm, the restaurants. How's that for something really superficial? But, the restaurants. A place to eat and you can get good food now in the Twin Cities. Whereas, when, when I was growing up, everything was canned. Uh, the first McDonald's raised a stir. Chinese was... like Chun King, and now you can get Thai, you can get...you know, it's like, we're like the rest of the country, I guess. We've joined the world. Fresh salmon. Good stuff. So, better food. Better food and

better roads. And you can always tell what's happening in a city by who's drivin' your cab. And, we've had such a huge influx of, thanks to the Lutheran Church, of course, of uh, of both Thai folks and Somalis, and whatever, and it's made us all much more interesting and, and maybe conscious of our fellow man, I think. That we have some differences and some language changes. And the foods, the language, the culture– all of that just makes the city richer, I think.

What's stayed the same?

The Lutherans (sigh). The uh...

Is that a good thing, or bad thing?

(Laughter) I don't know...some things just stay the same. The same Lutherans. Garrison Keillor's the same, thank goodness. Uh, although he talks about sex a little more

Dog Walking Mears Park, oil on canvas, 16" x 20", plein air

Farm Fresh

than he used to. The lakes are still beautiful. Uh, one of the things I love about St. Paul is that, unlike Minneapolis, instead of tearing down a building, they make something else out of it. Like, they made this building into my apartment. In Minneapolis they rip it down like at Grant Park, and they put up some great big monstrosity instead, where I have friends living. And so does Al Franken, by the way. He just took a condo in Grant Park. And, so we know that he's thinking about coming.

Looking out twenty years in the future, what kind of changes do you see?

Rapid transit. Uh, much more diversity in this town—much, much more. We were just talking about the future over at the restaurant there; that, in fifty years maybe there'll be more peace because we'll all kinda be the same skin color n' the same hair color, n'. . .

Yeah, and someone pointed out, uh, an old Star Trek episode where there was a guy that was black on one side, and one on the other. . .and the other one was. . .and they were the last people on their own planets, and they were still fighting. So I don't know if that'll change anything. But, uh, I don't know. We'll see. I'll be dead, so. . .I don't

know. There'll still be people in the park. Like, I get a loaf of bread out to the birds about once a week. Someone'll still be doin' that, I'm sure.

So what keeps you in St. Paul?

Uh, St. Paul is very relative. I can walk everywhere, and get from here to there on foot if I need to. I can always talk to someone who knew someone else, who knew someone in St. Paul. It's small enough, you know, and, and Garrison always says, "Good ole St. Paul." But it's just, it's this big, little town. That it's just big enough to feel like you're not locked away, and it's small enough that you can get everywhere and you can meet people. People are friendlier here. People don't move around as much. Uhm, you meet people all the time in St. Paul, who, they're forty years old and they have a house that's two blocks from where they grew up, and their folks still live there and their sister lives down the street. You know, that kind of thing. I like that. I was living in Uptown for thirty years, twenty years, and I just looked out the window one day n' thought, I can't grow old gracefully here. Got to go to St. Paul. Not as much blue hair and piercings.

What would it take to get you to move?

Out of here?

Out of St. Paul.

To where? It depends on where, I suppose. I don't know. I'm very happy here. I've looked at condos, 'cause I'd, I would like to be here permanently, and I can afford a ridiculously expensive apartment, but I can't afford a small condo in St. Paul, and I won't move out of the downtown, so that's the problem. But, I don't know. I love it here. I turned down a job a year ago, a wonderful job in Washington, D.C. It was like twice my salary, and I was *this* close. And then I let 'em think I was gonna take it, and then the day before I was supposed to tell 'em finally, I, I just couldn't go. I had to stay here. I've fallen in love with this city. And you should think about, maybe, moving over here. You're in a great neighborhood, though. You're in one of the best neighborhoods of Minneapolis.

Well, I'm born and raised in Minneapolis, so. . .

Well, I mean, I was too!

Yeah, well, I haven't found my way out of it yet. So, any other thoughts, or things you'd like to share?

They're both great cities. Uhm, I know that you're doing your grant on the river, but water's the same. You know, it draws people. And what I miss about Minneapolis is when I lived out on the lakes, and I could. . . I walked around those lakes endlessly, and I biked around 'em. And, and I loved that about Minneapolis. But St. Paul does have the rivers. So, that's all.

No Market Today, oil on canvas, 36" x 60"

Well, thank you very much.

Thank you.

K.S. (Jit) Bhatia

Age: 54
Owner Maharajah collectibles shop
Saint Paul, Minnesota

August 30, 2005

Well, Jit, thanks for spending some time with me.

Oh, not a problem at all! I mean, I've been wanting to, so this is cool.

How do you pronounce your last name?

bah-tee-ah.

bah-tee-ah? Where were you born?

Uh, India.

How did you come to Minnesota?

Just traveling. Just met some people from Minnesota and decided to come over here. I met them in Europe.

Where'd you meet them?

Europe. In Luxembourg.

Anybody else in your family come with you?

Jit Bhatia building

I came by myself, but then the family came in, you know, ten years later. I was just like nineteen years old and I met this girl from Hibbing, Minnesota. And, I had such a great time with her I decided to come over here.

So, what happened to the girl from Hibbing, Minnesota?

Oh, I don't know. I never met her again. But that was just, you know, I ran into her over there so I just came over here.

How did you end up in St. Paul?

Well, she said Minnesota was a nice place, so I came to Minnesota. I didn't even know it was twin cities – Minneapolis and St. Paul. I didn't come to St. Paul. For fifteen years, I'd say, or ten years I was in Minneapolis most of the time, but I did go to St. Thomas. So I would never cross past St. Thomas – never came downtown. And then, now I have my business here, so we've always been in downtown. And there is a difference in the two towns, I can tell you that.

I came here in 1970.

1970 you came? You said you went to school here – St. Thomas?

The College of St. Thomas.

Did you ever graduate?

Yes.

What's your degree in?

Business.

What kind of family do you have now? Are you married?

I just got divorced, you know, I was telling you. I just got divorced after twenty-five years. My wife decided she didn't want me

any more, you know. So, I've got two kids, a boy and a...my boy is nineteen, and I've got a daughter that's ten.

Is the nineteen year old still here in town?

Yeah, he works with me over there. And at U of M, he is doing his second year starting this year.

How did you get your business going?

Just started, you know, I wanted to do...I wanted...I come from a business family. So, after college, I worked for Dayton's, and then I decided to start my business, as a joke. You know – it just started.

Why don't you kind of describe your business?

Fixing a Hole

On Seventh Street, oil on canvas, 20" x 16", plein air

It's just a gift store, you know, and we, we carry a little bit of everything. We've been doing it for, uh, twenty-eight years now, approximately. Everything from jewelry, gold, tee shirts, posters. I mean, you name it, we got it.

Yeah. It seems pretty unique to me.

Yeah. It's very unique. It's just that I'm a pack rat. I enjoy buying stuff. I don't have any bad habits other than buying.

Other than buying?

Yeah – ha, ha, I love buying. I'm into art. I mean we have... I told you, uh, I deal with a lot of artists. So that's why I always have this... I like artists. It seems like they never have any money, most of them I know. So, no, but that's good. The way I look at it, so, you know, it's just really smart that they are more into their art, than trying to collect money, to make it big.

When you think of art, what does that mean to you?

Whatever I like. Whatever turns me on. Like, I buy art. It started out more as a business deal, because I knew art is a, a good investment, you know, most of the time, so I started with my posters and all that? I have always been enamored by, uh, printed pictures. From day one, even when I was in India, I used to buy posters all the time, and so I've always bought, you know, prints and posters and all that. So, I have stuff from India. I've got stuff from Thailand. I've got

Hand Sorted

stuff from Europe, you know, so wherever I go, that's one thing I do, is pick up posters.

Do you have a favorite piece?

No. I mean it's like, just about everything. I mean it's you just like you can't pick one kid, you know, so to me they're all favorites. There's always certain pieces, you know. Pieces that I bought in the beginning are the best for me, you know? I mean, I bought

Jerry Garcia, his original art. I have a lot of that. I bought, you know, a piece that I bought, uh, that is Salvador Dali, that I bought twenty years ago. You know, things that...I, I like everything. But, my thing is just more owning it than enjoying it, because I have so much of it. You never have problems. So, now I'm starting to change that part. That's why we, you see the store, how it's changing, you gotta, you know, know how to separate things. So it's hard.

But not everything stays in sight.

Looking back to when you were nineteen and came to Minnesota, what were your first impressions of the Mississippi River?

Yeah, well I didn't even know the Mississippi River went through here. When I came, I had no idea. Period. And, I'm not a water guy that much, you know, I mean this is a land of ten thousand lakes? So I enjoy going to all these places, but it wasn't where... I didn't go over there for the water part of it, it was more to see people, you know, I just enjoy it. I love talking. I love making friends, as you know, so this was a fun part of it. So, I have no impressions of the Mississippi. I just knew that Mississippi separated the, is it the Mississippi that separates the two, or is it the Minnesota? Oh, uh, St. Paul and Minneapolis.

The Mississippi.

So, what changes have you seen from when you came over as a nineteen year old to now? What other... the town and the people?

Well, I mean, the town's gotten bigger. You know, uh, I'll tell you one thing, I *love this town* – both of them. I love Minnesota is what I should say. The, the friendliest people I've ever, ever met. Okay, I've been here thirty-five years altogether, right? I don't think I've ever been discriminated – ever – that I can tell. I could be, I'm too stupid, you know. I just don't feel like, you know, that there's any reason

Rain or Shine, oil on canvas, 24" x 36"

for anybody to discriminate, you know, being from India, and all. I'd just take it for granted that everybody loves me, and it's worked for me. And there might have been people that didn't care for me, but I, you know, I... I'm just too stupid to understand, you know, from the vibes or whatever. But I just do my thing. I just keep goin'. I love, I love this state. I think that it's just beautiful.

So, it's gotten bigger, but what would you say has stayed the same?

I think, uh, you know, uh, uh, the feeling. What I felt for this town from the beginning, is still there. The town is beautiful. The people are very friendly still. You can still walk...I can still walk down the street and make friends. I don't think you could do that in a lot of other towns. I haven't tried a lot of states, because this is where I spend most of my time. But it just feels like a, a, like St. Paul, you feel like a small town feeling. I know everybody in town, I mean, I just walk down the street and I know everyone. I mean, where you gonna get that?

Do you live close to the store?

On the Job

Right now I'm living upstairs, but I'm moving back to my old house. But I've always lived in the suburbs, but when I got divorced, I moved over here, and, and I'm using one of my apartments. And, next month I move back.

If you were looking out twenty years from now, what do you think this area will look like?

It's gonna be more like Minneapolis, I think. It just seems like the way this area is going with all the housing and all that...going on the river, and add the shopping coming in, Xcel has already changed a lot, downtown. A lot more people are interested in St. Paul. I always thought of St. Paul as the deadest town, you know, because there was just ne... never anything happening. But in the last six years I think things have changed quite a bit, since Coleman was the mayor, eight years, you know? Things have been a lot different than what they were. It feels more exuberant. More people are excited about Minnesota, about St. Paul. I can just feel it with people when I talk to them.

Do you view this as a good thing, that it's changing for the better?

Oh, I think so, yeah. I mean, you don't want to see... most ...all over the country, I think, the downtowns are dying. And I think that just the rebirth of downtowns, I've seen that happen to Minneapolis, twenty years ago, and now I'm seeing the same thing in St. Paul. And I've always believed in St. Paul. That's why I bought so much, you know, I

Order Up

own a lot of property here. I think it's future is good.

What keeps you here?

I just like it. This is my home. Why do you say home? Because this is where I feel grounded.

Have you lived any place else?

I've lived in India. You know, I lived all over, so, and, I mean, I've traveled all over the world, so... I shouldn't say all over – more western countries in all. I've been to Thailand, I've been to India. I've been to Hong Kong, been to Philippines, you know, but those were in my young days. I've been to Europe *a lot*. I still go there all the time, but, this is what I think of as home. When I come home, you know, I mean I don't know how you feel, but when you're away it's always fun to come home. When I come over here, it just feels like, you know... here... I'm

done. It's a good feeling.

What would it take to get you to move?

I won't move, I mean not, not that I can see. I mean, if I went through my divorce and didn't move, there's no god-damn way I'm moving now. No, there's just no way. This is my home base. I still travel a lot. I still plan on traveling quite a bit. But this is where my home base will be. No. This is my home.

Have you seen any changes in the use of the Mississippi River? How has that affected you?

It hasn't stopped growing yet. It hasn't affected me at all. And, it's for the better. We should use the Mississippi. But, I couldn't tell you. It hasn't affected me either way. As I told you, I'm not a water guy. So, doesn't, it's not like I go hang around the Mississippi River to watch the boats and all that. That

At the Landmark, oil on canvas, 16" x 20"

doesn't turn me on. I'm more interested in running my businesses. You know, this is what I enjoy! I enjoy my customers. I make a lot of friends through them. I mean, that is what's been, you know, the best thing in my life, is my businesses. Because I meet so many unique, different people. That's how I met you, right?

That's right.

So, that's what I look forward to.

Well, that kind of finishes us up unless you have any other thoughts or comments.

No. This is something you want to do. I just want to hang around with you and talk to you about your business.

Brie Kindy
Age: 24
Waitress at Patrick McGovern's Bar & Grill
Saint Paul, Minnesota

August 10, 2005

Tell me a little bit about your family and growing up.

Uhm, both my parents, my dad's from actually St. Paul. My mom's from, uh, Minnetonka, I believe.

Any brothers or sisters?

I have an older brother who was born, also, in Minnetonka, and a younger sister who was born at North Memorial, so, in Crystal.

Where did you go to school?

I went to Cooper High School, out in New Hope.

So, all public schools?

Yup. I went to an alternative school for the

Brie Kindy

last two, two and a half years. Which was the Highview Alternative. It's right by Cooper.

Any school after high school?

I went to Hamline University for a couple of years.

When you were growing up, if you can kind of think back to your first thoughts of the Mississippi River, do you have any memories of that?

Uhm-uh, my dad is, uh, a huge, huge water boat person. Uhm, he actually owned, he owned a construction company when I was little, so he had a, a boat that he kept on the St. Croix and Mississippi, and we go and we'd take it out every weekend that we went out there and, and so I have some memories of going up there on his boat and going canoeing and stuff like that, so yeah.

With the whole family?

Uhm-hm. Well, my, my parents are separated, but my dad and my brother and I, and his girlfriend or whoever would go also at the same time. But yeah. Lots of fun! Dropped the keys in the river once. That wasn't so fun, but (giggle)...But, it was a lot of fun. We, uh, just got back from sailing on Lake Superior, actually, this past weekend. So, very, very huge on the water. Like to be around it. Definitely enjoy it.

Thinking back, you grew up in what town?

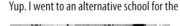
Potatoes and Tomatoes

Crystal. Yes, Crystal, Robbinsdale, New Hope, all those areas. And my dad was living in Delano for a long time and then he moved and he's now back in Madison.

And where are you living now?

I live in St. Paul. Off of like Hewitt and Snelling. So right, actually, by Hamline University.

When you're thinking back to twenty years ago when you were a kid, what do you think has changed with the town or the river or the people? What was it like back then?

Uhm, I think, I mean I don't remember anything, I guess, different about it. I just, I remember, well, other than you can't swim in the river. But, I mean, that was a huge thing, but other than that, I don't know. Seems the same to me. The river and the people. Always very friendly every time you go boating you're always waving, "Hi." And people are friendly once you're out on the water. And I think that's stayed the same, so.

Saturday Morning Market

Do you still do a lot of things with the river?

Uhm-hm. Still go out canoeing, and I'll go, uh, we just went sailing, and I'll go on the boats. I have a friend of mine who has a boat, and he brings it out to, like, Lake Minnetonka or something like that and we'll go out there. It's a lot of fun. Go down to, uh, the falls and go and watch the waterfalls, and walk along the little creeks and stuff. Still tryin' to hang out on the water!

Have you seen anything different in the Twin City area? From when you were a kid versus now?

Having to do with like?

People, transportation, environment, business, crime, anything.

Uhm, well, like at the falls? Yeah. You can't

go down there any more at night. It's just too dangerous. There's too much, too many people...

At Minnehaha Falls?

Yeah. You can't go down in there anymore. It's too dangerous. There's a lot of garbage and trash thrown out about that way, and it's not kept up as nice as it used to be. But, but...

If you're lookin' out twenty years from now, what do you think might be different?

The changes, hopefully, will be for the better – with cleaner environment, cleaner air, not as much trash, people actually picking up, stuff like that. But, uh, I don't...unless they get on it, I don't foresee, like I don't think that that's gonna happen – that people are gonna

take care of the stuff. So, back on the negative side, I'll say it'll probably be a lot dirtier and just...not as nice. You won't hang out by the water any more. More dangerous. More people going down there like, late at night and stuff like that.

If you had one story about an adventure around the Mississippi River, what would that be?

Uhm, well, there have been times, like, uh, we would take the boat out and we'd go on a little dinghy on the Mississippi River and we'd go through all the little canals and just go along the shallow water areas by the Mississippi – me and my brother – we used to do that. There was the time when we got off the boat and I dropped my dad's keys in the water. Three years later, the guy who had the slip right next to him found it, which was nice.

Oh, really?

Yeah. It was pretty funny. Yeah, he was fishing, and fished the keys out of the river! Uh-huh, so that was kinda funny and nice, uhm, is there anything else? The Mississippi's been pretty quiet, so we usually just go out, you know.

How often?

Oh, we used to go out every weekend 'til I was about thirteen or fourteen, maybe? So, quite a while. Yeah. So that was a lot of fun. Don't get to do it so much anymore.

Well, a little bit off the subject, because this

is an art project, when you think of art, what does that mean to you?

Uh, uh, I just think of creativity. That, that would be the first thought in my head, would just be creativity.

Do you do any art?

I don't have the creative, creative personality.

Do you know any artists?

No.

Not really?

No, not really. My brother's got quite a few friends who enter pictures and photography. He's got a good friend of his that took a bunch of pictures of, like, she went to Ireland, and she had pictures and stuff like that going. But that's about the closest I know to anyone who does any artwork, so. But my mom! She makes little bird baths and stuff out of rhubarb leaves! (giggles) But, (giggles) that's about the extent of it.

Smoking Section

Do you have any plans to move away from here?

Not yet, no. Eventually, probably.

What would it take to have you move away?

Uh, my dad is starting another construction company, so as he gets it started – he's in Madison right now trying to do it, so, if he gets it started, there's a good chance I might go down there to help him run it. So, just, just family business, that would make me.

Any other thoughts or comments you might have?

Uhm, nothing, really.

Are you enjoying working here?

Yes! Yes, it's a lot of fun.

So, you've been working at McGovern's?

Yes. I've been here for about four months now, and I left from Billie's on Grand, so, still Saint Paul area. I was there for a couple of years. I used to work, actually, at uh, Sophia, down in Northeast Minneapolis, right along the river. Yeah, and we'd get a lot of people coming in from there and a lot of the joggers and all that stuff, so, I used to get to watch the river every day. However, then...that's okay.

Talk To Me

Did you know a waitress named April from Sophia's?

April Rog? Yeah. A very good friend of mine. I haven't talked to her probably in a couple of years, but, yeah. She's really cool.

Yeah, she went out with my youngest son. They're very, very good friends.

Okay, well, if you talk to her, tell her Brie said, "Hi."

Three Sisters

Red Wing

Heading south from Pigs Eye Lake in Saint Paul, Highway 61 follows the Mississippi River for 38 miles, passing the Prairie Island Indian Reservation, to arrive at Red Wing. But before there was an Indian Reservation and before there was a Red Wing there were the Mdewakanton (born of the waters) Dakota tribes.

The Dakota met their first white man in April, 1680, with the arrival of Father Louis Hennepin. On September 18, 1805, Col. Zebulon Pike held a conference with Dakota Chief Hupahuduta (a swan's wing dyed red). Later in 1823, the name Red Wing was suggested for the settlement by U.S. Army officer Major Long. In 1837 and 1851 treaties took most of the land from the Indians and, after many broken promises and harsh treatment, in 1862, the Dakota fought back. The uprising ended with a mass hanging of 38 Indians in Mankato, Minnesota. The U.S Congress abrogated all treaties and the majority of the Dakota were moved from the state.

In 1880 some Mdewakanton families began to return and in 1936 the Prairie Island Community was given a small portion of the island for their reservation. Treasure Island Bingo was started in 1984 and in 1988, gaming gave the Mdewakanton a chance to rebuild. Treasure Island Resort and Casino has since grown to employ over 1,500 people and is the largest employer in Goodhue County, of which Red Wing is the county seat.

Red Wing, with a population of 16,020, has been able to retain the feel of an 1890s town. The historic downtown features gems like the Sheldon Theatre (built in 1904 and restored in 1986) and the 1875 St. James Hotel which features 61 unique rooms with great views of the Mississippi River. It also is home to the state's oldest county historical society, the Goodhue County Historical Society chartered in 1869.

Mostly white (Red Wing 94.3% vs. Minnesota 89.4% and the U.S. 75.1%), Red Wing has a strong German (35%) ancestry. The next largest groups are Norwegian (17%), Swedish (10%) and Irish (10%). American Indian tribes make up about 3% of the population. Median household income ($43,674) is slightly lower than the state median of $47,111 but higher than the rest of the country ($41,994).

While retaining its historic downtown, Red Wing has continued to be a working river town. The Port Authority operates a riverfront bulkhead for filling the barges as well as a two-site, 284 slip, marina for personal and commercial boaters. Trucks constantly bring grain to fill the elevators and trains for shipment across the country.

The historic train station at Levee Park on the river still provides passenger service as well as housing the Red Wing Visitors Center and Arts Association. Best known for its boots and pottery, Red Wing is truly a jewel on the river.

Mike Poole

Age: 54

Ceramic tile contractor interviewed at
Randy's Restaurant
Red Wing, Minnesota

June 24, 2005

Tell me a little bit about your background.

Well, I was born and raised in Red Wing. I'm a graduate from Red Wing High School. Have my own business. I'm a ceramic tile contractor. Married, four adult children, six grandchildren.

Any of them still at home?

My youngest son, he'll be 21 in November, he's still at home. The rest are all on their own.

Where abouts do they live?

They all live in Red Wing, fortunately for me. There are many occasions where there are six grandchildren at my house all at once. Three girls are all within fifteen months and that can be kind of hectic now and then.

So, did you ever leave Red Wing?

No, not as far as moving. I've worked all over the country. I've been away from home, I guess, at one point in 1990 or '91, I was gone for three and a half months. I guess that's the longest. I did Old Country

Mike Poole

Buffet Restaurants. One in Canton, Ohio, Fort Wayne, Indiana, Detroit. No, I've never moved away.

How'd you meet your wife?

Met her at the bowling alley. Here in Red Wing. Nybo's Bowling Alley used to be on Main Street. That's where I met her. She was five years younger than I am. She's a farm girl.

So, what brought her to Red Wing?

Her folks lived on Munson Hill, it's called, about nine miles from where we are right now, downtown Red Wing. She went to school in Red Wing.

You said you're a ceramic tile contractor? What other kind of jobs have you had?

Construction, mainly. Little odds and ends, you know. Back when I was younger, get laid off, I'd find a job for the winter, construction

98 Degrees in the Shade

would shut down, rather than draw unemployment. Basically, it's always been construction.

Any education after high school?

No, just our tile.

When you think of the Mississippi River, what does that mean in your life?

What does the Mississippi River mean? It meant employment for my father. My father worked for the U.S. Corp. of Army Engineers. I guess that was pretty much what it meant to me. During our growing up days, we never fished or did anything at all because that was my father's work. He was on the Mississippi five, six days a week and so when his time off came, the last thing he was going to do was head to the river. But, after I grew up, I owned a boat for quite a while and I spent a lot of weekends waterskiing,

having a good time on the river. When I was younger, again, after the youngest child was born, well, there wasn't much time for play. It was work, and so I sold my boat.

OK. Thinking back, you said you were 54?

Yeah.

And thinking back to when you were a kid, What is different about Red Wing than what it's like now?

Boy, almost everything. I was younger. Small. Everything was downtown. All individually owned stores, shops. We didn't have Wal-Marts, Targets and food chains. Basically had two banks, then First State Bank and Burnside became the third. But now there're banks all over. But, Red Wing still maintains it's beauty. The city really takes excellent care of the town. We're pretty much known for the beauty here in the Hiawatha Valley.

A Spot of Shade, oil on canvas, 24" x 36"

So, what hasn't changed then?

The people. Pretty much. It's a real friendly town. Easy to talk to people. Always willing to help. That pretty much hasn't changed, I guess. Other than that, Red Wing keeps on expanding, but the population doesn't grow.

How does it do that?

Maybe you can tell me? (laughs) I don't know. I mean, don't quote me, but I believe the population of Red Wing in the last twenty years has maybe gone up 15, 16 hundred, at the most. And we have 30 percent of the homes in Red Wing are 20 years or less. Of course, now they are building a lot of town homes and condos and so on. Yeah, quite a few people wondering, all the new homes keep on expanding, building, building, but the population never seems to rise. I don't know if there are that many people that are passing away or what, but it just gets, it's funny.

So, when you look at Red Wing from the river and you see a lot of industry, has that had an impact on you?

Well, there again, my mother worked for Red Wing Shoe Company for 29-30 years before she retired.

What did she do there?

She was an outside cobbler. She fixed the nicks and cuts, going through the manufacturing process with the leather. She glued and repaired them so they didn't become seconds.

So, she was actually working with the shoes.

Yes. Working with the shoes. All those Red Wing shoes, I believe the biggest industry in Red Wing. It was. They had some layoffs, so maybe they aren't anymore. Not counting the casino. They have a lot of employees.

If you're thinking twenty years from now, what do you think might change? What will Red Wing be like?

I'm really not sure. I see all the major players in business moving to Red Wing all the time. I see no reason that that's going to stop. So, Red Wing Port Authority is trying to get new businesses all the time. There have been a few that have left. It's obviously pretty good deals to companies to come in to town. Some real good deals. Industry, I'm sure, and also, in my lifetime I've seen Hastings become, more or less, part of the Twin Cities. More and more people are living in Red Wing, Goodhue

County area and driving to the Twin Cities to work all the time. I guess, twenty years from now, it will just be a far out suburb of the Twin Cities. They put a new four-lane highway in where there used to be two lanes.

Are there plans to do that?

Well, it's four lanes, leaving Red Wing. Now it's four lanes all the way to basically highway 316 going to Hastings. Then you have two lanes from there to highway 52 on 50. There again, it goes to four and, I mean it's significantly, made my commute time, a lot less. Most of my work, that I do, is in the Twin Cities area.

You drive up and back?

Up and back. Today I'm doing a house for a friend, his mother, 92 year old mother. I started last night. It's a custom shower and bathroom tear-out. Framing was all soggy, the common wall, wall opposite the shower was all full of

Boat Houses

mold. Otherwise I'd be there right now, but I have to give it 24 hours to dry out. And, I still am probably going to have to reframe the wall and I'm not a carpenter but I'm able to do it. It's pretty much, when I give someone a bid, I live with it. If I have to buy some extra material or extra time, so be it.

I did have to do the floor in the shower, but added $75.00 on to it. She's 92 years old, so I went upstairs yesterday and I asked her if, her son Sheraton Thomas, retired insurance agent, and I asked her if she knew what his telephone number was in Lake City, he has a cabin on the river.

She says, "What do you have to call him for?"

And I said, "Well, your shower floor is hollow and I just wanted to talk to Sheraton and explain to him that it's not stuck to the concrete floor."

And she said, "Well, I'm the one that makes the decisions here." She says, "I'm the one who's paying you, he's not. I want it done right. If it needs to be taken out, take it out."

OK, OK. I just, you know, dealing with someone that's 92 years old, you know, and considered elderly, and there's so many people around, you know, that take advantage, you know, I mean you just go in, every bid that I ever made I stick to it. Stick to it. Unless there's extras and I just wanted to talk to her son, you know, this is going to be an extra. I tell you that we need to take it out, but she says, "Do it right. Tear it out."

So, I met him down there and explained to

Fishing at the Levee, oil on canvas, 16" x 20", plein air

him about the shower being all moldy and had to take out the floor and told him what his mother said. "That's mom."

She sounds like a sharp lady.

Yes, she is.

What keeps you here in Red Wing?

At this point, I guess, my children and grandchildren, that's the only thing, and my parents, the only thing that keeps me from moving closer to the Twin Cities area lessening my commute. But, not with all the kids and grand kids here.

We've talked about retiring in Puerto Vallarta, Mexico. We go down there frequently and my wife says, "Well, we can maybe move down there for two or three months at a time in the winter, but it's just that I could never stay there for six months away from the kids and grand kids too long."

So, no plans to move away?

No, no. Not on a permanent basis. I guess maybe a couple months in Puerto Vallarta. We have great friends in Puerta Vallarta. I'm involved in a couple businesses down there. One's not too bad, the other one's not the greatest.

Are these in construction areas?

No, no. Puerta Vallarta is about a quarter of a million people and I'm in the tourism branch. I have a partner that's half Mexican and

From the Top of the Hill

half Swiss, graduated from the University of Houston, worked for the Forestry Department for a couple of years, visited Puerta Vallarta and went back, gave his two week notice and has been there ever since.

Got into the commercial sport fishing business. We own some sport fishing boats and his business plan was great and I invested the money and all of a sudden his business plan went by the wayside and he doesn't want to put the time or effort into the business that he's supposed to. So, the profitability is, well, I just hope I don't lose all the money I stuck into it.

Another one I'm in is a finance company

owned by a friend of mine from Slayton, Minnesota. He owns it and it's a great business, great business, and I've invested with him. And that is secure, I don't have to worry about that.

Changing the subject a little bit, when you think of art, what does that mean to you?

Terry Redlin. I guess that's the simplest answer for me. I have several Redlin prints. One first edition. I love the outdoors. Redlin is unique, all his buildings always have light in them. The different shades, the times of day, I truly, truly enjoy his paintings. Although I did purchase one for my wife, I can't even remember what the

name of it is, but it's the one with all the kids flying kites around the big tree, huge blue sky and there's a dog in it. But, it's the most unlike Terry Redlin painting I've ever seen. I've been out to the Redlin art center four times. I have paintings by Les Moss, also. Redlin's my favorite.

Any other thoughts or comments, maybe back to the river? If Red Wing had been not on the river, would it have made much difference?

Well, I don't believe my father would have stayed here. He was born here and after he got out of the navy, a couple years, three years later, he went to work for the Corp of Engineers. There again, he was up and down the Mississippi, down the Ohio, Illinois River. Close proximity to the river would have been part of my life.

So, how did all the kids end up staying here in Red Wing?

Well, I guess, occupation. My son is in the ceramic tile industry, also. He and his best friend started a company. Now, they've closed the company down. They've gone to work for a sub-contractor out of Hastings. My oldest daughter works at the casino. As does her husband. My youngest daughter is working at the Kwik-Trip and going to school. She hasn't decided yet if she wants to be a RN or now she's kind of looking at forensic science. So, I guess the first four years are basically pretty much the same whichever field.

My youngest son, twenty year old, well, he still lives at home and he hasn't decided what

Red Light, oil on canvas, 24" x 36", plein air

he wants to do with his life yet, just gets irritating at times. But he's not too bad. He's never been in any trouble of any type. He tends to be bit on the lazy side, I think. But, "Don't complain, he has a job. He has a job."

Well, I really appreciate your time. Good stories, they helped a lot.

No problem, no problem.

Brenda Balzer
Age: 57
Part-time employee at the Best of Times bookstore
Red Wing, Minnesota

June 24, 2005

How about a little background on where you were born, where you grew up.

I was born here. Grew up here. I see your next question, my parents were born here, too.

Tell me little bit about growing up in Red Wing.

Well, Red Wing was a, at the time that I was born, a pretty quiet little river town. It wasn't the tourist destination that I think it's becoming and maybe is at this point. We always used to complain as kids that there was nothing to do, well, we've learned, as

Brenda Balzer

we grew up, that there is a lot in Red Wing. I think some of my favorite memories, though, were like the parks, Colvill Park, growing up and making use of that park. It's right by the river, there was a swimming pool, still is, new one, but that was really a gathering place for kids.

They, the school system has changed a lot, gotten bigger. It was very, uhm , well, White-Anglosaxon Protestant at that time. Wasn't much diversity in Red Wing back then and I think there is more now which is a good thing.

And that was public schools?

That was public schools.

Were there also private schools then in Red Wing?

There was, and still is, Saint Joseph's Catholic School and that, at the time, was grade one through eight, it's one through five now. And

there was another Lutheran school, which is still in existence, Saint John's, and I think there are two other Christian schools that are now in operation.

You went to public schools?

Uhm-hm, uhm-hm. Yep, that was a different thing too, they had one building that was seven twelve. There was no such thing as a middle school and now, of course, there's a separate middle school building. High school is nine twelve.

So what do you remember about the Mississippi River as a child?

Well, I remember my dad taking me out fishing a couple of times. He liked to fish a lot, I didn't get to go all the time, but it was

fun. He, they had a little fishing boat, and a little later on, got a small house boat and I remember that really well, too. We used to go out, as a family, when I was married with young children, on that boat, and picnic and enjoy the river, so, I spent a lot of time on the river. I enjoyed that.

Do you have siblings?

Two brothers and a sister.

Older or younger?

Younger. And, I think they'd all say the same thing, they're all kind of devoted to the river, having grown up by the river. It was something we didn't appreciate as much as children, it was just always, it was there. Really appreciate it now.

Hanging Out

Main Street South, oil on canvas, 16" x 20", plein air

Hot Dog

So, did you ever leave Red Wing?

Yes, we did. My husband and I got jobs in north-central Wisconsin and lived in Wisconsin for about twenty-some years, and moved back when our youngest child graduated from high school. It's actually, really felt like moving home. This is home.

Where did you meet your husband?

In high school.

In high school, OK.

(laughs) Yep, we started going together when I was a sophomore. And he was a junior. We've been together a long time.

That's great! Your parents still here?

No, both of my parents have died.

So, what brought you back to Red Wing from Wisconsin?

Well, I had, we had moved to the River Falls area. River Falls is not very far from here. It's about a half hour's drive into Wisconsin. Jobs. I'd gotten a job in Elsworth, which is really close and actually my husband ended up getting a job there, too. And, we, because it was the same distance driving from River Falls, as it was driving from Red Wing, or it would be, we just decided we wanted to make that move when our daughter was finished with high school. We didn't want to move when the kids, we didn't want to disrupt them. But, after they were out of the home, that was the plan.

OK, so, there are two kids? A couple kids?

We have three.

And they are all out of the house now?

Um-hum.

Any of them in Red Wing?

No. Two in the Twin Cities, one in Cloquet.

We talked about your dad taking you fishing, anything you did with the river when you were, say, in high school?

Just going to the beach with friends. That was what we did in the summer. We would just gather our chips and kool-aid, our transistor radios and we'd head for a day at the beach, which we did a lot. There was boating, did a little bit of water skiing, but, not a lot, mostly it was just to the beach and just swimming. But we were using, I guess, the Mississippi a lot. Just, neat to have it right out the back door, practically.

Kind of looking back from when you here in Red Wing, as a child, now you're back as an adult, what has changed the most?

Well, I think there's really an emphasis on tourism now, and there've been a lot of neat things that have developed as a result. One thing that comes to mind, is the stops by the "Queens", as we call them. The Mississippi Queen, the American Queen, the Delta Queen. There's actually a committee in Red Wing that plans events for the people that stop here. A welcoming committee, they're called the Queen Bees. (laughs) So it's a big deal when the Queens stop.

Other changes? Well, as I mentioned earlier, it's definitely a more diverse community. There's a pretty good, it's becoming a bigger and bigger group of Latino residents and some Asian and there's also a black group, and it just wasn't when I was growing up. So that's a difference which I mentioned I thought was a positive. We have a, there's a festival in the fall called a diversity festival and there, I'm trying to think if there's connections with that and the river? They have booths and so forth, but I don't think anything at that time is set up down by the river.

There is an art festival in October that's generally held downtown and, within walking distance, but then there's one in the summer, also, that's actually held at Levee Park. So, and there are other events that are held down at the, well, like at Bay Point, they have the Mississippi Shuffle, which is the annual cancer drive. They have other things that, other celebrations, I guess, that are held down there, too. It's just a nice area. Between, it seems like most of the time those festivals are held at Bay Point but, occasionally they can be held at Colvill Park, too, which is on the other end of town, but it is still big enough for groups of people.

So, if you're thinking about how things are, how life was when you were younger, and how life is now, kind of forward yourself twenty years into the future, what do you think Red Wing will look like?

Well, right now there's, you probably heard about the discussion about development of the riverfront? And there's a local faction that's very against the development of the river. They want it to remain natural. And, so I don't, right now I don't know how that's going to come out. It's just, they're having meetings and developers are coming in with their plans, people are listening and giving input. I, there are some pretty powerful people that are against the development. So, I don't know right now who's going to win out.

How do think, if the development does go through, how would that change the character of the town?

Well, the area that they are considering for development is near Bay Point Park. I haven't studied it enough to give you a really good answer about that. I just, actually there was a big article in the paper last night and I haven't read it yet. I brought it with me to read and I haven't gotten to it. It just changes it from a natural area where people enjoy the wild life and so forth and the beaches that are there, to making it private and not as much use for the common person. You know, truly, right now, I couldn't say,

will it be, in the long run, a detriment? I don't know. It's a big river. There's a lot of areas, but as the opponents are saying, there's one thing I did hear, if it's sold and developed, it never will be natural again. So, I think it's important to preserve because it is special.

Rock Fishing

So what keeps you here in Red Wing?

Well, I do have one brother and one sister and their families that still live here. One that lives up in the Cities. We have other relatives besides this immediate family. And, being that both my husband and I graduated from

high school here, we have a lot of old friends that are still here.

What would it take to make you move away, or, are there any plans for that?

No, there are no plans for that. Especially with grandchildren on the scene, we don't want to move anywhere too far. And, this is really home. We've enjoyed living in the other communities that we did live in, but we felt like it was home, like Red Wing feels to us. So, I just don't see it happening, but who knows. I don't see it happening.

And then, one more question, when you think of art, what does art mean to you?

Oh boy, it's really a gamut of things. When I walk out the door and see the flower baskets, I think of art. But, I also think of good literature as art. I appreciate the architecture in this town. I think of that as art. The landscape, the scenery. The bluffs, the river. I guess all of those things. I just got back, not too long ago, from a trip to Italy. Talk about art. The painting and sculpture and so forth, it's just absolutely astounding.

But I don't, I mean, we have some wonderful artists in Red Wing, but I think, you know, when I think about art in Red Wing, the first thing that comes to mind is more natural. Even though I think we have wonderful artists, I just think of the natural.

Any other thing that you can think about, that might be an interesting story, or, how did you come to work in the bookstore?

Well, I just had, she opened last summer, and I just stopped by on a whim. I've always been a reader, a member of two different book clubs, and I just said, "Well, if there's an opening, I'm interested."

And she said, "Well, write something up." And I did and we talked and she hired me. So, that worked out. And I work just a few days a week, which is nice. A nice amount.

Ruth Nerhaugen

Age: 57

Writer for the Republican Eagle newspaper

Red Wing, Minnesota

June 22, 2005

Well Ruth, where were you born? Tell me a little background.

I was born in Sturgeon Bay, Wisconsin, but I grew up in Michigan's upper peninsula. I came to Minnesota in the mid-1970s and lived in Red Wing for about thirty years now. My husband is from Goodhue County, so he's a life-long resident.

So, how did you meet him?

He was in the Air Force serving at a base in upper Michigan during the Vietnam era.

Ruth Nerhaugen

If you were both up in the U.P. how did you come back to Minnesota?

He wanted to return to Minnesota, which was his love, and Red Wing is only 25 miles from his home town. He wanted to be in a different town, probably, but back in Minnesota. He loves it here. A Minnesota boy.

Where did you get married?

We were married in upper Michigan, had a child there. He was still in the Air Force when we got married so did that for awhile.

Do you have other children?

We have one son that lives in the Twin Cities.

At least he's in Minnesota, that's kind of nice. So, where did you go to school?

I attended Northern Michigan University but only for two years. The local daily paper offered me a job writing and covering the University, so I left school with the idea that I would return, but I never have made it back to get my degree.

So, you have a lot of writing experience and real-life experience?

Yeah, I've been writing full-time for daily newspapers since 1966. With a few years off, raising my son.

You're the Arts and Entertainment Staff Writer, so, what does art mean to you?

Superlative

That's an interesting question. I guess I think about it in the practical sense because for me arts means the stories that I'm writing about for the arts page. It means our theater, local theatrical productions. It means music, concerts, outdoor concerts and it means the visual arts: the painters, the photographers, the people who create things, and we just have a lot of that going on in Red Wing. It's a very artistic community.

Well, when you got here you were a lot younger, when did you come here?

Here in 1975. I didn't start at the paper until '76 though.

OK. So, do you have any stories about your connection to the Mississippi?

To the river. We bought a house with a view of the Mississippi River. When I grew up on Lake Superior, and when we first came here, I was not very impressed by the Mississippi River. I remember I was at work here in the spring and someone came running into the office and said, "The first barge is coming!" and I said, "Barge? You get excited about a barge?". I was used to the ore carriers on Lake Superior and we used to just sit and look at Lake Superior.

I never learned to swim because it was too

cold. You would have frozen to death before you would have finished your lesson, but, I always loved looking at Lake Superior. The Mississippi River is, you know, kind of dirty and it's slow and kind of narrow here and you get barges instead of boats. So, I was not too impressed and yet, over the years, I've come to appreciate what the Mississippi River means to people who live on it.

By living on it, I mean on the shores of it. There are people who live on the river, too. A lot of boaters. People just like being out on the water doing things, but having the river running through your town means more than that. It's been a life-line for the community. It made it the wheat capital of the world at one time. People enjoy sitting, looking at the river every bit as much as I enjoyed sitting, looking at Lake Superior, and I've come to enjoy that, probably, just as much.

Any particular stories?

About the river?

Well, what are you doing tonight?

We're going to the park by the river to have a bonfire. We're not boaters. I've been on the river a few times, going on some of the river boats. Absolutely love going on the big paddle-wheel river boats, and the river brought those to town. You know, not every town has access to those things. I just sit and watch it. I've written about the river a lot.

Yesterday's News

I've covered art shows about the river. I know all about the disasters on the river. There's a disaster on the river where 98 people were killed on the Mississippi just south of here. But, the river is just kind of there, part of the town. It's one of the attractions, one of the things that make you feel at home.

What changes have you seen in Red Wing since 1975, thirty years ago?

There have been tremendous changes. And yet, a lot of things have stayed the same. The dispute, right now, over what to develop or not to develop along the river, people in town don't want their view and their access of the

river to be denied and sold to some in a big condo who's going to pay a lot of money for it.

So, what was different about it thirty years ago to now? Could be the town, could be the people.

Let me think for a minute. I think that the town has discovered it's uniqueness. Covering different aspects of the community for the paper, when I covered city government I was fortunate to cover when they were doing some historic preservation, and that has been very successful in the past 30 years. They've taken some of the old buildings and adapted their use or just fixed

them up and they're using them again. The St. James Hotel is an example of a wonderful restoration. The Sheldon Theater, wonderful restoration.

I think, when I came here, take the Red Wing Pottery, the first pottery convention was 1977 and, at the time, people just thought it was so funny that people from other parts of the country were interested in that old Red Wing pottery that everybody had a bunch of in their basement and they had crocks on the porch with flowers on it, that sort of thing. Now, these pottery collectors come from all over the world practically, and they'll pay thousands of dollars for this old Red Wing pottery that was never anything special. It was just part of Red Wing.

The Sheldon Theater was just always there, and it was a movie theater for a long time. Well, that's fine. It was there. The St. James Hotel, worked just fine. People were happy that things were just the way they had been. And yet, when they began to realize that these things were threatened or endangered, buildings were going to be torn down, and we had to lose a couple of buildings, I think, at one time, our mayor sued the city council, sued the city, to try to stop the demolition of what we call the Irish row houses because nobody really realized they were in danger. And they had to think about it, "It's just the old Irish rows houses, you know. How valuable, how much do they mean to you?" But, over the course of perhaps a decade, people came to realize that what we had in Red Wing was very special, but you needed to protect it and you needed to put money into it. And then you come to appreciate it.

I think when you almost lose some of those special things is probably when you appreciate them more. But now, the Sheldon is gorgeous. The Anderson Center is being completely restored and Red Wing is very proud of it's historic preservation efforts.

So you say that restoring the feel of the buildings is what has changed the least or stayed the same?

I think that restoring them, and in doing so, giving the community a kind of pride in stuff that it was taking for granted, is maybe the biggest change.

OK.

Because people wouldn't have bragged about any of those old things, you know, when I came here. And now they have a different view of what is here.

Well, looking towards the future, what do you think the place and the people are going to be like in twenty years?

I don't think it's going to change very much. I think that the core community will continue to try to preserve the community as it is without stopping progress. We've lost a lot of industrial and manufacturing

jobs. And everybody knows you have to have jobs. You have to have jobs, so you can bring in families. You have to have families, so you can have kids and keep your schools going. We've closed four or five elementary schools in the past ten years because the school population is down so badly. That's happening everywhere. Plants aren't just moving into towns. It's very hard to maintain your economic base without accepting some changes and compromises. And I think they will continue to do those things to compromise and to allow change, which has to happen. But, we will never be a strong, industrial based community again. We will never be an agricultural community. Never has been, never will be.

I think for Red Wing, what will happen, it's not going to grow very much and I hope it's not going to shrink very much.

Well, you've been here thirty years, what keeps you here?

We love Red Wing. It's a nice small town with a strong sense of itself. A strong value for what it offers. And, at the same time, it's only an hour away from the Twin Cities. We raised our family here. We will probably retire here in a few years. My husband is with the school district and has valued that career. He's eligible for retirement and hasn't retired yet because he's having too much fun. But, he loves his work and I love being at the paper here. I can go anywhere

and ask questions and bother people and I love the arts community. I love the things that go on and I'm very close to them because of covering them. I'm having fun doing it still.

Are you an artist?

No. No. Artists, you need audiences, appreciators.

Well, writing is an art.

I know. But that's the only thing that I do and I don't really consider what I do an art.

Have you done any other kind of writing, or just reporting?

Mostly just reporting, a little free-lancing, but I started writing a column two years ago and that's a real outlet for me. Able to have an opinion after 28 – 30 years of not having an opinion of my own.

What is your column about?

My column's called the "Sunday Driver". Some people in town refer to it as my travel column. It's just a column that Sunday drivers pretty much go anywhere they want and do what they want. They amble along. They don't have deadlines. They just have a good time. Talk about anything they feel like talking about. I'm having fun with that.

Is that in the weekend edition?

Yep.

What would it take to have you move away from Red Wing?

I don't know. It would have to be a powerful attraction to be somewhere else. It wouldn't be that we didn't want to be in Red Wing. If our son relocated, if I was on my own and chose to move near other family members, it would have to be a powerful attraction to be someplace else. It would not be a city. It would be a small town like this where a person can just relax and enjoy life, drive from one end of town to the other without getting into a traffic jam.

Any other thoughts or comments, concerns, insights?

It's a very Scandinavian community, which you may find interesting.

You had mentioned Norwegian before.

A lot of Norwegians and Swedes. Actually, one of the things I haven't mentioned is that we have, two things, it's always been a diverse community because the Prairie Island Mdwauketon Dakota tribe is in the city limits. They consolidated with the township back in the '70s to bring the nuclear power plant onto the city's tax base. The nuclear plant paid two-thirds of the city's tax base for many years, but now they're working with the legislature so they don't have to pay as much tax so that's affecting the community. But, not as dramatically as people feared that it would. We've had a Native American population, but there hasn't been a very close connection between the Red Wing down here and Prairie Island until more recent years.

Now, in the past, probably a bigger change than anything else, and I haven't mentioned it, is the diverse cultures that are moving into the community. Red Wing is, it was a pretty white community. It was Scandinavian. It was German. But, people who want to get out of large urban areas and find places like this to live, because they appreciate them as much as we do, have come to Red Wing.

Unfortunately, not everyone that has come to Red Wing has fit the pattern. We've had more problems with, well, you don't just take somebody from a big city and plop them down in a little town like Red Wing. They aren't necessarily happy with it because we don't have the kind of attractions that they're used to and it's changed the business. We have neighborhoods with a lot of transient population.

We have people coming out of big city schools that don't have, haven't had a very good background education and they have trouble melding into

our schools just because their education programs weren't as good as ours and we have an excellent school system. So, Red Wing is struggling a little bit with the diversity issues. And that's going to continue because this is a very attractive community. It's a very nice place to live. Other people want to live here, too. And you can't close off.

One of the things that they've said about Red Wing for years is that it does not have a four-lane highway to the Twin Cities. You have to come on two-lane roads for awhile to get here. And, when I came here, people would tell me, "Oh yes, but they're trying to get those roads". After a couple of years you realize that they were doing everything they could to keep those roads from being built because they didn't want to become a bedroom community. It's way too easy if you are all four-lane and Red Wing is not a bedroom community. We have people commute, but this is a town. It's a community on its own with a strong city government, a strong sense of what it is. So,

that hasn't happened and yet these other changes, I think that we have to learn how to do better by them, to hook up with some of those other cultures.

Never did a very good job with the Native Americans, I think, until the casinos came in and started to develop a relationship. I mean our history with the Native Americans is terrible. We just pushed them off the land. Now they have their own land and a much better relationship than we had.

Weed Picking

One last quick question? Where's the best place to get breakfast?

Breakfast. My favorite place closed down. We've got a Perkins.

How about a family owned, Red Wing owned, mom and pop ?

Well, you'd probably like Bev's Cafe, in the middle of downtown. Oh yeah, that's the place you'll want to stop because you've got some of the retired gentlemen will have their little coffee tables in there and they're in there every morning and at Broschler's. Broschler's is a bakery and cafe and they have excellent food.

Winona

Paralleling the Mississippi River as it flows southeast towards Iowa, Highway 61 takes you 55 miles from Red Wing into Winona. Winona is squeezed between the river and what was once the main channel of the river, Lake Winona, with the bluffs of Garvin Heights overlooking it. Once the largest city in what became Minnesota, Winona has a population of 26,641.

Before the arrival of white settlers, the area was the home to the Mdewakanton Dakota (Sioux) tribes led by Chief Wapasha. The first person to write about the area was Zebulon Pike in his log book on September 14, 1805. Forty-six years later, on October 15, 1851, riverboat captain and owner Orrin Smith dropped three men off on the sandbar and laid claim to the riverfront and surrounding prairies. Originally named Montezuma, the named was changed to Winona (first-born daughter) in 1853.

Because of its location at the intersection of the railroads from Chicago and the Mississippi River, Winona grew rapidly. Over 1,300 steamboats stopped in Winona in 1856 alone. They carried grain and lumber to the rest of the country. In the 1860s Winona was the main port for shipping Minnesota wheat and southern Minnesota was the largest wheat producing area in the country.

As the railroads grew, so did Winona. With the completion of the Winona Railway Bridge which opened on July 4th, 1891, Winona became one of only two places in the country where trains could cross the river. Growth continued until the collapse of the

lumber industry and Winona's population, after peaking in 1900 at 19,714, started a several decade decline.

Winona's strong European background still shows in its current makeup. With 35% of its population having German ancestry, 12% Norwegian, 12% Polish and 10% Irish, Winona is still predominantly white (94.5% vs. Minneapolis / Saint Paul 66%). The newer waves of immigrants that have settled in the Twin Cities have just started to reach Winona.

And while the median household income ($32,845) is well below the Minnesota median ($47,111) and national median ($41,994), Winona is still a good place to live because housing costs (median value $89,800) are also lower than the state ($118,100) and nation ($111,800). This keeps Winona affordable.

The river has always been central to Winona. Throughout the 20th century there have always been fishing shacks, boat houses and house boats clustered on the banks. On Latsch Island in the middle of the river there is a large marina and there are several permanent house boats where people live on the water year round. Eagles can be seen soaring above the river hunting for their next meal while people fish from their boats or from shore.

And now, in 2006, with the planned Maritime Art Museum of Minnesota, a proposed river-themed history and art museum, Winona takes another step towards reinforcing its connection to the Mississippi.

Fishing Latsch Island, oil on canvas, 24" x 36"

Mitch and Alex

Mitch Gonsior and Alex Volkman
Ages: 15 and 14
Fishing the Mississippi from Latsch Island
Winona, Minnesota

June 15, 2005

Were you born here?
Mitch: I was born in St. Paul
Alex: I was born in Winona.

Related?
Mitch: Just friends.

Got any jobs yet or do you just like fishing?
We mow lawns over in Wisconsin. We know this guy's got a trailer park. We got fork lifts up there with a plow on it. We plow snow in the winter.

So, do you have your license yet?
No, but I'm getting my permit.

So, how often do you guys come down here and fish?
I've been coming down here every day for the past two weeks.

How long have you lived in Winona?
About a year and three months now.

What brought you down to Winona?
My mom just wanted to get away from her old husband and all the bad things that happened in the past.

Do you have any brothers or sisters?
Yeah, I've got two brothers and a sister.

Are they older or younger?
They're all older.

So, they're done with school?
One of my brothers is and my sister is.

Do you like it down here?
Yeah. It's peaceful usually.

Do you like school?
Alex: It's alright.

What grade are you in?
I'm going into 9th.

So, that starts high school down here?
Yeah.

Are you looking forward to that?
Not really.

No? Why is that?
I don't know. All the stuff that people talk about. A lot of fights and stuff.

Oh, really.
Yeah.

So, are there gang problems or anything like that down here?
Some people wannabes.

So they put on an attitude? Well, it's pretty mellow out here. Alex, how long have you been fishing?
First time I ever fished was when I was like 4 or 5.

Was that with your folks?
With my grandpa.

Do you have brothers or sisters?
Yeah, I got one brother and one sister.

Are they older or younger?
Both older.

How long have you been out here today?
Mitch: Since three (2 hours).

And all you caught is a turtle. What do you usually fish for?
There's lots of bass. Ten, fifteen feet over here. And walleyes and sheephead. Lots of catfish.

Boat Sweet Home

Steamboat Days Sunset, oil on canvas, 36" x 60"

So, do you eat them?

I don't like eating fish but my mom and them do. So, I always bring them home for them. If I catch any.

You said you guys were interested in art?

Mitch: A little bit. I like drawing stuff.

Alex: I'm not really a drawer but I like the stuff that my brother draws and his girl friend and his girl friend's mom.

What are the drawings like?

Like cartoon characters and stuff. Snow White and the Seven Dwarves or whatever.

She has them in her book. She should be around in a little bit.

Mitch: My brother, he like draws pictures of rappers and stuff.

So, he likes hip hop?

Yeah.

What do you guys plan on doing when you're done with school? Are you going to stick around Winona?

Mitch: We're moving in like three weeks here. Going to Spooner, Wisconsin.

Are you moving, too?

Alex: Not that I know of. Trying to get out of the housing, but I don't know where we'll move after that.

Houseboats on Latsch Island

Mitch: I just like being out in the country and stuff. It's peaceful. You see a lot of birds out there.

Kinda fun to watch the tug boats, That's what caught my eye as I was coming over the bridge. I saw all of the tug boats.

Mitch: There's been this really big eagle flying around the past hour. I guess it's gone now.

Anything else you guys like to do with the river?

Swim in it. There's a beach over there.

Is it getting warm enough to swim?

Yeah, I think it's really warm right now. Not too bad. (Mitch is standing in the river)

At least the top 5 inches.

Steve Strelow and Doug Beeman
Ages: 54
Two city works employees doing stump removal, interviewed at Beier's Restaurant
Winona, Minnesota

June 17, 2005

Steve, you said you were born here, raised here?

Yes.

So, how long ago was that?

54 years ago. 1950 I was born. Went to school here. Worked here all my life. Raised a family and live out on the river, out on Prairie Island. It's called an island but it's actually a peninsula.

Are you originally from Winona?

Yes.

Your family still here?

What's left of it. Yeah.

What's your connection to the Mississippi River? Got any memories about growing up?

Hunting, fishing, swimming, boating, all that kind of stuff. Still do a lot of duck hunting and fishing. Always been on the river, ever since I was a little kid. Learned to water ski and stuff like that. Doug and I did a lot of fishing years ago together.

Doug Beeman and Steve Strelow

Cleaning Up, oil on canvas, 16" x 20", plein air

So, what kind of fish do you get out of the river?

Doug: Walleyes, sunfish, crappies. Them the ones you usually fish for. Along with your sunfish and crappies, but there's sheephead, there's catfish, northern, there's sturgeon. All kinds of fish.

Steve: Small billed catfish. Lot of rough fish, buffalo.

Doug: But mainly it's the pike and the pan fish that a person goes after. Ice fish and fish during the spring and the fall, you know that's your best fishing.

Do you get your kids out there fishing? Do you have kids?

Yeah, I've got two daughters. I've taken them fishing many a time when they were little, you know, but not so much now. They've got their own life going on.

How old are your daughters?

23 and 24.

Are they still here in town?

Oh, yeah.

Well that's nice.

One's an RN and the other one's a beautician.

They have a good nursing school down here. Did she go to school here?

She went up to Duluth, University of Minnesota, for the first year then down here to finish it off. But, yeah, they got a good school here.

What have you seen in Winona? How has it changed in the last 30 years since you guys were kids?

Steve: It's grown a bunch. The sign doesn't indicate that the population has changed much, but things must be changing because they have a big, comprehensive plan for the upper Mississippi wildlife refuge that Fish and Wildlife wants to change a bunch of regulations and there's not, (pause) some of us old school people aren't too happy with their ways of thinking. But, there's been some pretty heated discussions and meetings along the river past couple months. I went to a meeting a year and a half ago, and I just couldn't believe some of the restrictions they want to put on the river because of the basically over-crowding.

Have you noticed over-crowding? Is there a lot more traffic, more use of it?

More people fishing. More people have boats, you know.

Doug: They make it so easy to get a boat now days. You know, give me the boat, no down payment for a year and $29 a month for the next 10 years.

Steve: It's really crowded.

Doug: They make it too easy and everybody's got a boat and everybody's out there, especially on the weekends. Mostly pleasure, but there's a lot of them that fish, too.

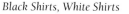

The marina on Latsch Island, has that gotten any bigger or has it changed? Are there other marinas?

They spruced it up. Put new dockings in and all that stuff, but, and built a bigger area so that they can store them in the winter time, but as far the harbor itself, it's always been about the same size. They could use one just as big again, you know.

Steve: But, 30 years ago, when we used to fish, you know, we'd go on the weekend and there'd be 15 – 20 boats fishing below the dam and now it's just...

Doug: Years ago you had a secret spot. You could go somewhere and there was nobody around. Be there all by yourself. Now you go there, there's six boats, you know. There isn't no secret spots no more. Everybody's in there.

Steve: There's a lot more commercial traffic. They're gonna dredge the commercial harbor over here. We're gonna dredge that and make more room in there. There's a lot of...

Does that mean more tug boats, more barges?

Sure.

So, looking down the road 20 years, what do you think it's going to look like? What's going to happen with your environmental wildlife studies?

There's going to be a lot of restrictions. I mean, I don't know if you've ever heard of that comprehensive plan, it's 800 some pages and it's gonna be tough for us old-school people

Black Shirts, White Shirts

A Sterling Crew, oil on canvas, 24" x 36"

because the good old days are gone. As far as, if they only put half of their proposals into action, the good old days are gone.

What kind of things would be changing?

Well, they're gonna change some of the refuges like for migratory waterfowl. They'll restrict some areas to non-motorized boats or crafts. They're gonna, (pause) normally the government in the good areas where the ducks and stuff, what I'm concerned about is the better parts of the river that you can still hunt, or is somewhat productive for hunting, they're gonna take some of those places and turn them into refuges and give you a spot that's basically no good to hunt. For example, up by Wabasha, there's the Tiffany river bottoms and dike splits from Wabasha to Pepin, below that you can still hunt. There's a refuge above Elma, but there's an area in between that you can still hunt. It's basically a pretty good area to hunt. They want to take that away and want you to hunt Tiffany bottoms. So that's what I'm concerned about. Shortening the season, only let you hunt until noon, instead of all day. They're gonna limit you to 25 shells. Things like that. So, they're looking at a lot of stuff.

Is their intent that more people hunt, or that more people are already out there and they want to cut back on usage?

They're looking at 15 years down the road, just like you asked, you know, what's gonna happen in the next 20 years. They're looking at population increase over the next 15 years and figuring that it's changed quite a bit in the last 15, they're just looking ahead. It's just hard to, change is hard when you used to be able to follow a few basic laws and do what you want to do, but things have changed a lot.

So, how often do you guys get out to fish or hunt?

As much as we can fishing.

Doug: To hunt, usually quite a bit.

Just like after work kind of fishing type stuff?

Yeah, that's about it. After work or if you got a vacation, you take a couple days off work, you know, get out there and do a little bit during the week. Weekends it's pretty hard to get out there. There's so much traffic.

Steve: Most of the people that fish like to get out during the week instead of the weekends. There's so much traffic that it's tough. It's real tough.

Well, changing the subject a little bit, do you have any connection to art? Or, what does art mean to you guys?

Prints, you know. A few prints or things like that. Waterfowl, mostly for me.

Doug: Usually animals. Waterfowl, bear, deer. That's all I've got hanging on my walls.

Steve: I've got a few prints of, I can't even remember the name of the artist, but a real

Ice Cream Social Time

nice print of a big old colonial style house with a bunch of kids out on the pond skating. You know, things like that. I like stuff like that, but most of the stuff I have is waterfowl prints.

Do you know any artists? Any of your kids ever show any interest in art?

No. You're the only one we know.

Well, hey, it's a start. Well, what are you guys up to today?

Well, we work on a tree crew grinding stumps. We remove trees and trim trees. We're out removing stumps today. We cut one down a few years ago, Lake Park, where the band shell is, we cut a huge cottonwood down there a few years ago. Biggest one we've ever cut. Nine and a half feet in diameter.

When you talk about grinding a stump, normally they're cut down so they're ...

Looking Down Third Street, oil on canvas, 16" x 20", plein air

We cut it down as low as we can to the ground and use a machine to grind it. Haul the chips away, bring back dirt, put it in the hole.

So, would you mind if I got some photos of you guys grinding a stump?

Doug: No, that's alright.

Do you know where you are going to be?

Steve: A bunch around Grand Street, I think.

Sharon Lunde

Age: 59
Volunteer at the Winona Visitors Center
Winona, Minnesota

June 15, 2005

Sharon, tell me a little bit about where you were born, how you grew up, a little background.

I was born in Winona and I was raised here. It was a great place to grow up in, neighborhood's really close-knit. Lot of children, we all played together. It was great. I don't think that happens so much anymore, but it did then.

Are your parents from here, too?

Yes. Well, my mother was born around... my mother was born in Medford, Minnesota, I think, and my step-father was born in Winona. And uhm, it was just a great place growing up. I loved it here. I still do.

Do you have any siblings?

I have one brother.

OK. So, local schools. Have you always lived here?

Yes. My daughter was raised here also. She did go to college here, too. Lisa graduated from Saint Mary's College and then continued her education in the twin cities.

Has she given any thoughts to moving back?

Has she?

Yes.

Not with her profession. She's an attorney and she is not crazy about losing her life to private practice. She works for a corporation in the

Twin Cities and she works 40 hours a week, period. So, she doesn't make extremely high wages, but she has a life, too.

Have you ever lived any place other than Winona?

Nope, born and raised.

OK, and what did you do after school? After high school. Well you got married. So, how did you meet your husband?

I met my husband, back in that genre people, young people, kind of hung out in the downtown area. And this cute guy was riding past on a motorcycle and I thought he was really cute and I waved at him. He stopped. Took me for a ride on his motorcycle.

Unfortunately I was wearing a skirt. But, it worked out. (laughs)

Maybe that was one of the attractions.

Could have been.

My husband was born in western Minnesota. He has lived here since he was 12. He worked out of Winona for many years. But drove back and forth to his jobs. He was a construction ironworker and the majority of jobs were in the Rochester / Twin Cities area. But, he liked to be here at night. It was just better than staying in a motel for him and eating out all the time. That's it.

OK. So, what did you do then?

I had a variety of jobs then and, when we had our daughter, I stayed at home with her. I worked part-time off and on a little bit. But I stayed at home with her for many years.

OK. So, when you think about the Mississippi River, what are your connections to that? Do you have any stories to relate? Time spent on the river?

Just that I love it. I love living by it. I love being able to see it every day of my life, if I want to. I love seeing the big Queens moving up and down the river. I like seeing them walk through the locks. That's fun. And there's a lot of boat traffic, but I guess my, the things I really like the most, are the big Queens. And we have two of the three that travel up here and we may get the third one

Sharon Lunde

back next year.

Where do they travel from?

Mainly Saint Louis. To St. Paul and down and back.

Well, in all of the time that you have lived here by the river, what would you say has changed the most?

About the river?

About the community, about the people. Life here.

Because of the times, we have some unsavory elements in Winona that we didn't have before. Simply because they didn't exist before. Drugs are more prevalent. But, the one thing about that is that it really doesn't, the average citizen doesn't know anything about it.

So, it doesn't impact the average person's life.

Not really. Only the dealers and the ones that are on drugs or buying and selling, and that's a really, really small percent of this community.

So, do think that wasn't there, or maybe was there earlier but you didn't notice it because you weren't affected by it?

I don't think so because I don't think it was ever public and I think that our city officials have been pretty forthcoming in what is going on in our community.

Looking Good

Is this methamphetamine?

Meth and cocaine. There's a lot of marijuana too, I understand, but for me personally I, I don't know positively, but I'm not that concerned about marijuana use, I guess. But, cocaine and the major heavy drugs, I am. And meth, especially.

Well, that has been a change. But what has stayed as kind of a constant?

The beauty of the area. The friendliness of the people.

OK. Do you have a lot of long-term friends that have lived here?

Oh, yes, friends that I've had for 30, 35, 40 years. And they are still around, and if

they're not, we communicate by phone, e-mail, you know, visit.

Looking 20 years out, what do you think might be changed?

In Winona?

In Winona.

You know, I really don't think that any of the big things will be changed. I think it will still be a beautiful community. I think it will still have friendly people. I think we'll still have our student base here, I don't think there's going to be that much of a change in twenty years because I don't see that much of a change. There've been changes, but not major changes.

How about, you have a Wal-Mart now, right?

Yes, but I don't have to shop there.

But that hasn't changed the feel of the city or the feel of the people, the connections?

We used to have a lot of locally owned businesses. That part has changed. And, like every other community in the last few decades, malls have been built in outer areas where there's more room. Downtown areas in a lot of communities have lost businesses, we're no exception to that. I miss, I really, really miss, the smaller, locally owned businesses. And, we used to have tons here. And we have some now, but certainly not the way it used to be. It's all chain stores and malls. Or box stores.

The same restaurants in Minneapolis as there are in Santa Fe as there are in Winona.

Isn't that exciting.

Yeah. Makes you want to go travel.

Yes, it does. Especially for the good dining.

What would it take to get you to move from here?

(long pause) Or isn't that in the plans. It doesn't sound like it is in the plans.

It's not in the plans to move because I will probably grow old and die here in Winona. But, the one thing that could make me move, is if a long-lost, wealthy relative that I don't know, so wouldn't be horribly distraught over their demise, left me money. A year-round place on a lake, in mid-to-northern Minnesota.

So, you'd move further north?

I'd move further north.

Do you like the winters?

I don't like the winters but I like cooler weather in the summers. And, in the winter, I hibernate during the winter. Lots of reading. I'm not into winter sports. Like all Minnesotans, we have a lot of down, a lot of polar-tech, a lot of sheepskin, this kind of thing to stay warm. But that's the only way I would move.

OK, one question which I kind of missed is, what does art mean to you?

Art to me means the availability of a lot of different forms of art. Whether it's plays, all kinds of different plays, wall art, whether it's photographs or different paintings, fabrics. Art.

Do you have any friends that are artists or do you do anything, are you artistic?

No, I'm not. And I don't have friends that are artists, but I do admire a lot of what I see at art shows and different craft shows. The better ones. I know it when I see it, but I could never do it.

So, thank you very much for your time.

Jerome Christenson
Age: 53
Opinion page editor at the Winona Daily News
Winona, Minnesota

June 16, 2005

Where are you from?

Ah, southeast Minnesota, well they call it that.

OK.

Family started out in Ostrander, which is nearby Spring Valley. They still back there. Actually grew up down, went to school, high school in Caledonia, Houston County. Then end up in Winona to go to college, back many years ago.

Which college here?

Winona State. Carefully selected.

Close to home.

Close to home. Knew that it was cheap enough that I could afford it, no matter what. And, that I wouldn't flunk out. That was very important when I went there because the last student draft deferment issued was on June 30th, 1970, which also, coincidentally, was my 18th birthday. (laughs) I carried that 1A card in my wallet long enough. So, there was a motivation there, too, to attend Winona State.

Jerome Christenson

So, after school, what did you do?

After school? Well, I stayed in school as long as possible. That scene in "Animal House" with John Belushi laying on the floor, "Seven years of college, down the drain." That resonated.

And this is undergrad?

Oh yeah. We don't want to get into that high-priced graduate tuition. I gave that some thought every time I approached graduation it was, "You know if I graduate and I come back, they're gonna charge me double, and none of these people are going to get the slightest bit smarter."

Did you get your seven years out of it then?

Oh yeah, I had a good time and it was well worth it. So I graduated with a degree in history and, of course, that's a career path if there ever was one. Especially going into the Reagan recession.

So, I went to raise hogs. Another brilliant career move going into the Eighties. That was down in Spring Valley / Ostrander. I was in that with my dad. In that until '85 when the Production Credit Association decided that we no longer knew how to raise hogs, so we shouldn't do it anymore. We concurred. So I went back to Winona 'cause I could get the same part time job I had in college. (laughs)

So you still knew some people here?

Oh yeah. Made pizzas. I was looking around for other jobs, and for lack of honest work, I found myself in journalism working for the paper down on Second Street that we don't mention anymore.

What were you doing for them?

Writing. A column. Reporting, occasionally fixing the press when nobody else could figure it out. It was a smaller operation.

OK.

I started with the Daily News about five years ago, almost five and a half years ago, now.

What kind of connection do you have to the Mississippi River?

Well, other than falling in it when I was younger, and living next to it for a good chunk of the last 30 years, I guess that's the biggest connection. Caledonia was a river town transported 20 miles inland. Half the town had boat houses over on Lawrence

Lake, so, everybody was running to the river on weekends, summer after work. So that was it. Grew up paddling along it.

Dad never managed to have a boat. He could never figure why you would want to own a boat when you could rent one over at Lawrence Lake. I tried to point out to him, that if you owned a boat, then you got a much bigger one that was gonna be a lot more impressive to the girls. Which didn't mean a whole lot to him.

So, I take it you own a big boat now?

Ah, no, no, no. I got married, so I don't need to impress the girls anymore either. (laughs)

Do you have any kids yet?

I got two. And both of them are grown, with business cards. That's wonderful. Erik's still in town, he works for Wells Fargo. Erin is out in Los Angeles. 23 and 25. She's the older and she spent five years in Germany. Decided she didn't, she always wanted to, all the while she was growing up, be somewhere else. No matter where she was.

You've been on and off in Winona for a long time, what have you seen? What's different now than 30 years ago?

Not that much, really. Which is surprising. You look at the town and a great deal has changed. I mean, everything over by Mankato, that was all marsh and a driving range. Where Wal-Mart and Fleet Farm and all the big boxes was a driving range. Where

K-Mart sits, that was just marsh and swamp. The little suburban developments up in the valleys weren't there. Back then the levee, the permanent dike hadn't been built yet. We still had the temporary dike from the, left over from the '65 flood, sitting down there being ugly. The Wilkie actually would float.

That's the name of the steamboat out there?

Yeah, well it was originally the Pearson. It was a genuine work boat that was a, a perfect example of the corrupting influence of money. The historical Society in '56 acquired this, the last wooden hulled work boat operating on the Mississippi. And they brought it to Winona, beached it, and ran out of money.

How do we restore, how do we preserve this old, it was the Pearson. And it was a squat little stern-wheeler work boat. Well, there was the president of the Historical Society, and you'd better do some fact checking, but he was in touch with Leighton Wilkie, who's father, I believe, was from Winona. I don't think Wilkie spent more than 20 minutes in town in his life. But anyway, he had the chance to do something wonderful, so, he made a bunch of money with the Do-All Company, which was a tool company up in the cities. So he had more money than he knew what to do with.

So, he said, "Well, I'll help you out. Help you restore this boat."

And then he looked at the boat and said, "I don't like that boat. That doesn't look like a

steamboat. That's not a real steamboat. A real steamboat looks like what you see in "Showboat". In the movies. Let's get some frilly smokestacks up there. Let's get a super-structure. Let's paint it white. Let's make it glisten, and then, let's name it after my dad."

So, we got the Julius C. Wilkie. Which was all plywood and fake woodwork attached to the wonderful, old Pearson, that was a genuine.

And they parked it down on the levee and it sat there until 1980, when they had to move it.

In the '65 flood, they were really concerned that the old boat was going to float away in the flood. So they chopped holes in it

To sink it?

So it would fill with water. Basically, they scuttled it on dry land. Had they not, it would have just lift up off it's moorings and down the river. Which probably would have been better.

In '80, they had to move it because the permanent dike was coming through. So, they're moving it off the site and then they're gonna move it back. Ah, well, somehow it caught fire. Total loss. So, what was a genuine historical artifact, had first been bastardized, then it was burned, and then Leighton Wilkie noticed that, "Gee, my dad's boat isn't there anymore". So, in a great flurry of public sentiment, and another pocketful of Wilkie's money, they had this tremendous fund drive and in the space of just a few months, rebuilt the Wilkie. Put up this boat shaped building

down on the levee that you saw. Which is neither fish nor fowl nor nothing else.

It wouldn't float.

It doesn't float.

But, it's not in the water, so it doesn't have to.

It's in the concrete. It's not gonna have to be scuttled if it floods. But the real problem with it is, nobody, to this day, knows exactly what to do with it because, Mrs. Wilkie wanted a grand ballroom. So the second deck, up there, is all red velvet and plush. I mean, it's done up like a New Orleans whore house. And it was supposed to be a cafe. Well, trouble is, they didn't have a kitchen or running water or any practical accouterments.

So they'd have to have a catered event or something.

But, it's cold and drafty and the whole thing, it's got a, you know the deck is bowed as steamboats were supposed to, so it's really difficult to walk on. Particularly if you have a catered event where you've been catering alcohol. Makes walking funny.

Immediately after they got the thing done, it started to rot away. It'd leak. It's just been a disaster.

Makes for good stories though.

But, it's Winona landmark, so you can't get rid of it. And, so far, nobody's managed to sneak up there with a can of lighter fluid and a Zippo and do the good deed.

So, in other words, 20 years out, when we're envisioning what Winona will be like, that will still be there.

Maybe it won't. There's hope. They're bringing the dredge in, the William S. Thompson, that will be part of an exhibit. And this is backed by smarter money with a certain amount of integrity.

So, what other changes do you see might be happening in the next 20 years?

Well, I don't know. Winona State has grown explosively. The look of the town has changed dramatically. But, the feel of the place is pretty much the same. It's still a freaky little river town.

A lot of interesting little shops, still.

Well, interesting little shops and interesting people. One of the things that really attracted me to Winona was when I was in high school. Down in Caledonia, they had a (for kids who could read, and there were few of us) a special "come on up to Winona State and we'll learn ya something" day. And that's about all I remember of the formal part of it, except you got here and one of the presenters was a member of the history department at Winona State, Henry Hull.

I had never encountered anybody like this. He stood about this high. Shaved head. Full beard. Walked hunched over like this. Kept drinking out of a thermos jug, which, being naive, I thought was coffee until I sat next to him at lunch and, nope, that's not coffee!

But, he had this great, raspy voice, "My name is Henry Hull."

And, in the space of a very short time, Uncle Sam not withstanding, he pretty well made up my mind that I wanted to go to Winona State 'cause I had to figure what the hell he was all about. He was just, just a character! And I got here and discovered this whole town was full of characters. It was just freak heaven in the '70s and it really hasn't changed much.

Strutting Their Stuff

I keep thinking they'll die off and we'll drift into normalcy. But no. Somebody else pops on you and you see them, now that I've been here long enough, I can see them growing, reproducing themselves. But that's the amazing thing.

Used to be said a few years ago, Winona was great. We had an old Saber jet, Korean War Saber jet at the kiddy land park.

I used to go climb on that.

We had the Saber jet down there. We had the Wilkie. We had the boat that don't float, the plane that don't fly and the nun out of order.

Sister Lillian. Lived out of her car and rummaged liquor bottles out of the bishop's trash so she could point out that he was a man of sin.

I missed her.

Oh, she was wonderful. Sister bicycle. Good old Lillian. She made hardened editors flee, literally. When I was at the Post, there was a code, that if Lilian came to the front desk both the editor and the publisher and anybody else, was out the back. (laughs) She'd just take forever and not take "no" for an answer.

Ellory Foster, who was gonna change the world out of a little office on Second Street. Old, old, ancient fellow. And the thing about these guys is, they could write forever. And always on lined paper and with wretched penmanship, and just keep showing up. And, eventually, the guy was about in his 80s, drunk on his ass, got hit by a car and killed.

Not a bad way to go. What's your position here?

I'm Opinion Page Editor.

So, you're looking for people that have opinions, I bet.

That's not hard to find in this village.

If you can think of anything, are you planning to leave Winona? What would make you move away?

Earthquake, pestilence.

So, you're a lifer.

Yeah. I've got no reason to go somewhere else.

What makes Winona really special?

It's about as eccentric as a midwestern Norwegian boy can handle. It's just a hot little, quirky place; endlessly amusing.

EXHIBITION SCHEDULE

May 2, 2006 through May 27, 2006

Robbin Gallery
4915 42nd Avenue North
Robbinsdale, Minnesota 55422
763-537-5906

June – July, 2006

Red Wing Art Association
418 Levee Street
Red Wing, Minnesota 55066
651-388-7569

August 1, 2006 through August 31, 2006

Minnesota State Arts Board
400 Sibley Street, Suite 200
Saint Paul, Minnesota 55101
651-215-1600

October 16, 2006 through November 17, 2006

Sherburne County Government Center
13880 Highway 10
Elk River, Minnesota 55330
763-241-2700

November - December, 2006

Paramount Theatre and Visual Arts Center
913 West Saint Germain
Saint Cloud, Minnesota 56301
320-257-3112

Index of Paintings